# The Vile PLACE

## Damaged by the System

NIAMH CONLEN

authorHOUSE®

*AuthorHouse™ UK*
*1663 Liberty Drive*
*Bloomington, IN 47403 USA*
*www.authorhouse.co.uk*
*Phone: 0800.197.4150*

*Published by AuthorHouse 12/07/2017*

*ISBN: 978-1-5246-8325-2 (sc)*
*ISBN: 978-1-5246-8326-9 (e)*

# Contents

Chapter 1    Family ................................................................ 1

Chapter 2    Lizzy ................................................................. 5

Chapter 3    First School ...................................................... 7

Chapter 4    Grief And Loss .............................................. 12

Chapter 5    11 Plus .............................................................16

Chapter 6    The Vile Place ................................................18

Chapter 7    Teachers ......................................................... 24

Chapter 8    Weekend ........................................................ 27

Chapter 9    The Mirror ..................................................... 32

Chapter 10   Going Down .................................................. 37

Chapter 11   The Sick Note ............................................... 42

Chapter 12   Netball ...........................................................45

Chapter 13   The Ruler ...................................................... 49

Chapter 14   Blood Invasion .............................................. 52

Chapter 15   Abba .............................................................. 54

Chapter 16   Summer .......................................................... 58

Chapter 17   The Tent .........................................................61

Chapter 18   Sinister ........................................................... 63

Chapter 19   The Hospital .................................................. 68

Chapter 20   Bridget ........................................................... 71

Chapter 21   The Choir ...................................................... 77

Chapter 22   The Stairs .......................................................81

Chapter 23   Down Again ................................................... 84

Chapter 24   Storm And Kerry ........................................... 89

Chapter 25   Snow And Abba ............................................. 94

Chapter 26   Heart Attack .................................................. 97

Chapter 27   C Group And Francine .................................. 99

Chapter 28   Periods ......................................................... 106

Chapter 29  The God Father ..........................................110
Chapter 30  Medicated ...................................................112
Chapter 31  Nail Polish Remover ...................................114
Chapter 32  Human .......................................................117
Chapter 33  Needlework .................................................119
Chapter 34  Final Days ..................................................121
Chapter 35  Conclusion..................................................123

# Chapter 1

# FAMILY

Once upon a time, on a bitter cold January night in a Lancashire mill town, a young man named Sean Conlen made his way through the deep snow to the maternity wing of the hospital, where his baby girl had just been born. It was 1964, and in those days, men did not stay in the delivery room while their wives gave birth. It wasn't the 'done thing'.

"She's beautiful," he said proudly in his gentle Irish accent.

The baby girl stared quietly at her loving parents with wide open eyes. It was as though she was in deep thought from her first day, weighing the situation and wondering who were all these people making a fuss of her arrival.

The young couple named their new arrival Niamh Conlen. This little girl couldn't have been born to better parents. Her father, Sean, worked from dawn till dusk seven days a week in a miserable textile factory, a dead-end job far from the beautiful green fields of southern Ireland where he had grown up. Niamh always regretted that her father never made anything of himself. He was a very handsome, charismatic man who could sing like Frank Sinatra and Tony Bennett. He could have been famous if he had wanted to be, but he just worked and worked to give his family a nice life. It was a waste of his talent and inhumane that a man had to live in a dull, windowless building doing a repetitive job day in and day out, looking forward only to the two weeks a year when he had a holiday. Growing up, Niamh became hugely resentful as she heard her father say repeatedly that working class folk do *not* live; they just exist. He was a socialist and despised the unfair class distinction and the vast gap between rich and poor. All he wanted was a cottage back in Ireland with some land and ponies for his girls and lots of cats, dogs, chickens, and goats.

But in middle age, as he finally attempted to fulfil his dream, Sean was struck down with cancer and died at the age of only forty-six. It was a very bitter pill for Niamh to swallow. So, she thought, life was for the rich and famous, who live long and happy lives; her father died young because he wasn't rich and famous. She developed a hatred for the royal family and all the rich and famous. Why did her father die? Why weren't they rich? Why wasn't her father a successful businessman? If he had been rich, then he could have had better treatment for the cancer that ravished him, and maybe he would have lived to a ripe old age. Why did he tire himself out making some rich bastard mill owner richer and richer while he became weaker and weaker!

Niamh's mother, Kaitlyn, was equally beautiful, with raven-black hair and olive skin, but she too wasted her life and talents. She was a brilliant pianist and taught the piano in her spare time, before she was married, and the children came along. She was also a trained hairdresser and qualified nurse. With all these opportunities, she should have been more than another factory worker in a weaving mill with dawn-till-dusk hours. And later she worked in an exhaust factory, where she was subjected to toxic materials such as glass fibre and asbestos. As she had felt regret that her father lived and died a factory worker, Niamh also regretted that her mother did not exercise her potential qualities but settled for a dead- job also.

Mother and baby stayed in hospital for a good two weeks, as was the norm then for new mums. Her father got to work on the nursery, painting, decorating and fitting new carpets. He wanted everything to be perfect for his baby girl. The baby's maternal grandfather lived with the young family, and his presence added to the happiness of the little girl's life. She loved the security and comfort of having in effect three parents, and she grew up believing that every little girl had a grandad living with her.

Grandad was so excited as he waited for his new baby granddaughter to come home. Born in Dublin, Ireland, Bill had been a soldier in World War I, fighting to protect Britain, his mother, and seven sisters from the threat of German invasion. He was heartbroken at the death of his beloved younger brother, Tom, through a freak accident with moving aircraft. Tom was guiding incoming planes taxiing on the runway, and even though Bill had warned his brother time and time again to keep his head low during take-offs and landings, it fell on deaf ears. One horrible day, the family received the dreaded news from the army that Tom had been killed when he was struck by the tail of an outbound fighter plane and decapitated.

The trauma of being forced to kill or be killed in battle had caused Bill to lose his religious beliefs and his faith in human nature. Her grandfather's experience also affected Niamh's thinking in later life. Why was it that only poor people had to fight on the front line in wars? Where were the members of the royal family with all their medals pinned to their uniforms? Were members of Parliament on the front line? She quickly learned that money could take you far away from any war or poverty, and only the ordinary man in the street would be killed in the trenches.

The baby was home and settling into her routine with mum, dad and grandad Bill. One night Sean and Bill decided to go to their local bar and wet the baby's head, so brimming with pride, they told friends and their landlord about their precious addition. During the evening the landlord had his own announcement. His German shepherd dog had given birth in the night to a litter of pups.

"Can I see them?" Sean asked.

"Would you be interested in one?" replied the landlord.

After consulting with his father-in-law, Sean decided that it would be good for his daughter to grow up with the puppy. So a few weeks later, he chose the most stunning pup in the litter and named him Kubla after Kubla Khan the warrior, who was strong and majestic. Kubla was golden brown with long, fluffy hair and he and the baby adored each other forever. So began the love affair of Niamh with animals.

***So, what could possibly go wrong with a child born into a loving, stable home?***

# Chapter 2

# LIZZY

Three years passed and little Niamh's life was to become more enchanted with the arrival of her baby sister, Lizzy. It was Christmas Day, 1966 and her father, Sean, was walking his wife Kaitlyn to the end of their street to the waiting ambulance, which could not get close to the family home because of snow piled up six feet or more. Sean was strong and able to support Kaitlyn arm in arm until they finally reached the ambulance. Niamh's grandfather Bill and visiting uncle and aunt from Ireland were caring for the excited soon-to-be sister at home while her parents were on their way to a Lancashire hospital to await the arrival of little Lizzy.

Sean and Kaitlyn were proud parents again to a beautiful baby girl, but it was touch-and-go for mother and baby. Kaitlyn had a difficult labour, and she suffered a pre-eclampsia fit resulting from her sky-high blood pressure as she went into childbirth. When Sean realized that he could have lost his wife and unborn child, he made the decision that the couple would have no more children. It was too life-threatening. They had planned on a typically large Irish family, and Niamh would have loved more siblings, but the realization that she could have lost her mother and sister soon put that idea into perspective. She would on many occasions try to imagine what life would have been like for her with just her father and grandfather. She couldn't bear the pain and grief that might have been. She imagined that her father would die from grief and then her grandfather, she would be an orphan. "Horrible," she would say to her parents and sister as they discussed it in later years. "Just horrible."

**Niamh adored Lizzy and thought she was the best Christmas present Santa Claus had ever brought her.**

## Chapter 3

# FIRST SCHOOL

In September 1968, little Niamh started school. She was excited at first, but the separation from her mother was too much to bear so she broke down in an inconsolable convulsion of tears. It was heart-breaking for her mother to see, but she was powerless to do anything because attending school was the law!

By 3.30, little Niamh had had a traumatic day. The moment she saw her mother, she sobbed with relief to be back in the comfort of her loving arms.

As all children do, Niamh settled down into school life, even though she would have preferred to be at home with her mother. She enjoyed primary school life, the stories before home time, the magical nature walks, the Christmas and Easter activities and the long, hot summer holidays. Holidays were always spent back at the family home in Ireland with Grandmother, uncles, aunts, countless cousins and of course her beloved German shepherd, Kubla Khan. Tuam in County Galway was the family home and Niamh and her younger sister Lizzy would spend many happy hours in the ancestral home playing with cousins and listening to the gossip and the `Craic' coming from the adults, picnics by the river Curragh and pony trekking along the green fields and stone walled roads.

Another 3 years passed and Niamh would be moving up into the junior class and under the supervision of the very first teacher to physically assault her. Mrs. Graham was a middle aged, grumpy woman who stank of cigarettes, had a smoker's cough and only had one tooth in her head. She wasn't a patient woman and perhaps she was ready for retiring and just couldn't be bothered with teaching anymore. So, it was end of the school day at 3.30 and all pupils had to place their chairs on top of their desks for easy cleaning of the room by the caretaker, after this home time prayer's would be said. Just before Mrs. Graham would start off the prayers, a chair had fallen off one of the desks, the teacher didn't see the culprit, but she just guessed at the direction of the room by the sound. Niamh and a few others saw the chair fall *accidentally* but they never said a word to the teacher about who the chair belonged to. So, when Mrs. Graham asked "who has knocked their chair down? "nobody spoke, "I will ask you all again, who has knocked their chair down?" Again, silence. "Right! I will just have to guess at who the culprit is", she said sharply, then she walked right over to Niamh took her arm and struck her with a bamboo cane. After the initial shock, Niamh burst into tears and ran quickly to the school entrance where her mother was waiting to collect her.

Her mother was unforgiving and furious and immediately complained to the head teacher he rightly demanded an apology from Mrs. Graham and she reluctantly gave in. After that Niamh hated Mrs. Graham but she hated more the selfish boy, who let Niamh take the blame, even though it was an accident, but maybe he was too terrified of Mrs

Graham to do the right thing. Niamh was reluctant to give him the benefit of the doubt but seeing as he was a nice boy she halted her hatred for him after a few weeks.

***So, Niamh had experienced her very first physical abuse but this would be the first of several assaults at the hands of the 'education system'!***

A few months past and the pupils got the good news that Mrs. Graham was to retire, yeah! The children were over the moon "The Witch is dead" they would sing from the movie The Wizard of OZ. They were introduced to their new teacher Mrs. Lounge, a fiery red head with a fiery temper to match, it became clear to the children that Mrs. Lounge was 'Not Nice' and they were careful as not to upset her, she had a trick of winding her finger around a 'culprits' hair slowly then yanking it as hard as she could as punishment for disobeying her or daring to stand close to her with a runny nose, she would on many occasion ask the 'scruffy' pupil with head lice to stand ten paces away from her because she didn't want to catch whatever they had and she didn't mind telling them. She once literally tied a boy to his seat because he kept wandering around the classroom when he should have been doing his work. Another boy was so terrified of Mrs. Lounge that he wet himself while doing his sums, sat on his chair, when she screamed at him for an explanation the poor lad burst in to tears and stuttered "I was scared to ask you if I could go to the toilet in case you smacked me".

One day during a maths lesson, as usual Niamh was struggling to cope because she just couldn't get the idea of calculation, no matter how many times the teacher would repeat the instructions to her, it was a mental block! Mrs. Lounge was in her usual bad mood and suddenly announced that "the next person to get a sum wrong will feel my cane", yes you guessed it, the next person was lucky old Niamh. Hauled up to the front of the class, out came the cane and whack, right across poor Niamh`s little hand. Again Niamh cried and cried to her mother, it wasn't just the pain of the assault but the humiliation that the whole class knew that she was thick, but the class didn't laugh, they felt upset for Niamh, but they were also traumatised because they knew that they could be next if they got a sum wrong. Niamh`s mother, furious that her precious daughter had been assaulted yet again, went angrily to the head teacher, she was adamant of removing Niamh from the school, but the head teacher didn't want that because it wouldn't look good on the school **OFSTED** report would it! Or maybe he was truthful and sincere in his apology, well, we will give him the benefit of the doubt again! So, the offending teacher was forced to apologise, and she never harmed Niamh again, it was a good thing that Niamh`s mother wasn't a violent woman or there would have been some casualties in that school, seeing as it was **not** a crime to assault children in those days but it would have been different if Niamh`s mother had assaulted the b****** who harmed her baby, the police would have soon been called. Niamh always questioned why this was allowed, why was it allowed to hit children in school but if any parents revenged their child then they would be dragged through the Magistrates Court! Why?

*So, this would-be Niamh's second experience of physical abuse at the hands of the education system in the 1970s and she wasn't even 10 years old yet!*

Putting these two assaults on her person aside, on the whole Niamh loved her primary school days which were made happier at the start of her mother being employed as a `dinner lady' there. She would run to her mother every dinner time and anything that was on her mind that day i.e. school work or nasty teacher was soon put right by her mother's comforting words and cuddles. She felt confident and protected by her mother's presence in the dinner hall and on the school playground.

# Chapter 4

# GRIEF AND LOSS

Niamh had a terrible fear of losing her mother, her heart would break for her mother after hearing how she had lost her own mother to cancer when Kaitlyn was only 15 years of age. How cruel of God thought Niamh, to take away my grandmother from my mother so young. Even worse was the fact that the funeral was held on Christmas eve in 1955. The image in Niamh's mind is one of misery, on a bitter cold day which should have been filled with Christmas cheer, joy and peace to all, was filled with grief and deep depression instead of deep happiness. Why had God treated her mother in this horrible way? Her mother had been a perfect daughter, an excellent Catholic who believed in everything the Pope had declared to be true and every word in the Bible. So what was the point of pleasing God if this is how he repays you, how dare he cause her beloved mother Kaitlyn such pain and grief! This was the start of Niamh's questioning of God and Religion. "There can't possibly be a god, why does he let this happen? Why does bad things happen to good people? It should be the other way around, bad things should only happen to bad people," she would often say to herself and her parents, she would constantly question why?

Niamh was very bitter about her grandmother's early death and the pain and misery it caused her mother, her grandfather Bill was so inconsolable that he never forgave

God and never darkened the doors of any church again except to walk Kaitlyn down the aisle on her wedding to Sean years later. After her mother's death Kaitlyn had to give up her career as a piano teacher and work in the mills full time to put food on the table for herself and her ailing father Bill. Bill had been a very successful electrician at the local mill but became the victim of two jealous men who sabotaged his excellent work in the building and bring about his sacking. Bill knew he had done his job correct and he could not understand why sockets were shorting out and this caused him to have a breakdown. The intention of these two men was to make Bill believe that he was going insane and make the management think that Bill was `passed it`. All this on top of his beloved wife's death was too much for him and he gave up work and took to his bed, it was only the arrival of Niamh's father Sean who brought Bill out of himself and gave him his confidence back that he started to enjoy life again and when Niamh and Lizzy where born, well, that was the icing on the cake for Bill, he had a new purpose in life and the two girls became his life, he adored, cherished, worshipped the ground they walked on. As Niamh grew older, her mother would tell her of the heart-breaking story that caused her grandfather's sacking from the mill and she would also point out the culprits in the street to Niamh when she would see them in a shop or walking near the family home. Niamh despised these two men and she secretly hoped that one day her father would avenge her grandfather in any way that he thought fit!

# Interval

The author hopes that by now, you the reader has a good insight into the life of this young girl Niamh, she was from a loving, normal family, no problems at home, no physical or sexual abuse in the family, nothing to cause stress or unhappiness. On the contrary she had an enchanted childhood until she was forced to go to the school that she would despise all her life. If only the authorities had an ounce of compassion or understanding at that time and allowed her to go to the same school as her beloved best friend. In the authors view they, the 'powers that be' were whole responsible for the decline in her mental health and wellbeing. The fact that she did not achieve academically, the twisted view she had on life the distrust of strangers, always thinking there must be a hidden reason why anyone would want to befriend her, but the worst was the mental torment! The repetitive, constant rituals, the fear of losing her parents, the fear of contamination, the physical abuse from other pupils and ***teachers***. These bastards were meant to protect Niamh, she expected the low life scum who attended the school to assault her at some stage but never the teachers and for what? Forgetting a sick note, laughing with another pupil after the whistle had been blown during a p. e lesson, being the only one ***not*** to talk after the teacher had left the room, forgetting her p. e kit! In later life, she came up with the conclusion that these adults in *authority* enjoyed the power to assault children that they took a dislike to or even to show their power, but Niamh was never cheeky or insolent, she was the absolute opposite and she hardly ever spoke. On this basis, Niamh holds the council and teachers at the time totally responsible for her failed adult life! The fact that she did not have a good job or money to do the things that she always wanted, it seemed that everyone she knew had passed her by in the career or job respect, she felt left behind by people who she thought were never as clever as herself, that all she gained from school was a mental illness of OCD, delusions, hatred of people, and a fear of the town where the school stood. She could never visit the town at weekends with her mother as all mothers and daughters do on shopping sprees, no, not Niamh, she would spend Friday nights in the shower scrubbing herself clean from that vile place and she certainly wasn't going to contaminate herself on a Saturday. ***Unthinkable!***

# Chapter 5

# 11 PLUS

The years went by and suddenly it was 1975, Niamh was about to embark on her `11 plus'. This was the equivalent to today's `SATS' but it was cruel because if you failed it you were sent to the big rough loser's school instead of being able to stay with your best friend who passed the test and went to the posh, clever school named `The Covenant'. Niamh was quite popular at primary school and she had nice, loyal friends but Delia Fawcett was her best friend, she had an infectious chuckle and dimpled cheeks, the boys would chase the girls in the playground and they were never short of `proposals'. The childish love letters passed under the table when teacher wasn't looking "will you be my boyfriend?" and "you fancy Derek", such fun and laughs. So, Niamh was aware that if she did not pass this test she would be separated from her beloved pal because DF was a clever girl and it went without saying that she would pass the test. On the day of the test Niamh did her utmost to pass and it worked because she was a `Borderline' student which meant that she was just under the pass mark but if she passed the entrance exam to the Covenant then she was home and dry and off to the `winners' school with DF.

***The next step would be crucial in the moulding of Niamh's life and mental health.***

A few weeks past and the day of the entrance exam was nearing, Niamh had been ill with a virus which presented itself with recurring nose bleeds or was it the fear and stress of being sent to the `losers' school if she failed!

The morning of the exam was dull and rainy, Niamh felt quite ill, she was also worrying that her nose would bleed during the test and she would be embarrassed and sure as anything that is just what happened. The assembly hall of the school was filled with desks and girls trying to get their place in that place. Poor Niamh was too busy trying to stop her nose bleed from going all over her paper that she just could not concentrate, and disaster struck. She failed!

# Chapter 6

# THE VILE PLACE

The day before starting the 'Losers' school Niamh tried to make the most of her last day of happiness by playing out until well after tea time. She didn't want the day to end, she tried to be optimistic and studious and hoped that secondary school would be just like the adverts for the school with smiley faces and immaculate uniforms and everything you needed i.e. pens, pencils, compass and the money belt for your dinner tickets to be stored she quite liked the money belt and its design, she thought to herself she would be a model pupil and succeed and make her parents happy. That is all she wanted to do is make her parents and grandfather happy. She also wanted to honour the memory of her beloved deceased grandmother whom she never met and never would meet but held in high esteem in her heart and mind, she hoped that she was up in heaven looking down on her granddaughter and feeling happy and proud.

*So, Niamh would soon learn that the sickly adverts praising the 'vile place' posted on the back end of a bus were just propaganda after all!*

She spent longer in the shower that evening, the warm flow was comforting her mind which was running with fear and negativity of the unknown. What would the teachers and other pupils be like? Will she have to have a shower in front of them after P.E? All these uncertainties were running a mock inside her mind, there was nothing positive.

After what seemed to be the longest, sleepless night ever, morning arrived with the dreaded dawn. Niamh was so tired, and her tummy was churning, it was made worse with the smell of a full breakfast that her mother always made, especially with the onset of Autumn. "I'm not too hungry "said Niamh. Her mother replied worried "Aw darling, are you a bit nervous?" Niamh wanted to tell her mother just how nervous she was, but as always, she didn't want to worry her or show any weakness. After all, she was a big girl now, going to a big school. "You must eat a good breakfast darling, you will feel sick if not" said Kaitlyn. For a short moment Niamh felt like shouting at her mother to be quiet, she was irritated, pre-occupied with the day ahead, she had a bad omen about her new life at high school. She hated the situation, why did she have to go to this horrible place? Why couldn't she keep on going to her primary school as her mother did back in the day until she was 16? Her mood was darkened more with the fact that Lizzy her younger Sister was still attending primary school and Niamh envied her so much! Kaitlyn had no idea of what Niamh was going through and nagging her to eat wasn't helping.

After a half- hearted breakfast which she secretly fed to her dog and cat under the table Niamh walked wearily into the lounge where her mother had laid out all her new uniform warming in front of the gas fire, her mother always laid out both her daughters uniforms every single morning of their school life, always clean underwear, socks, and shirts as white and crisp as freshly fallen snow. Shoes were polished to a shine so fine that you could see your reflection in the black leather. Talcum powder and deodorant were the order of the day, teeth brushed to a gleam and hair fresh and clean. "Pride must abide" was her mother's saying as she looked upon her girls with pride.

Her mother and father drove her to the new school, she felt sick in the car and she feared she would throw up. The last few yards to the entrance gates were likened to 'Death Row 'in Niamh's mind, all she could feel was bitterness that she had been cruelly plucked from her little primary school and friends in the countryside to this marauding, ugly, dirty, fowl smelling building that was situated right next to an abattoir. For an ardent animal obsessed child this was horrific especially when the cross-country run went right past it, with the smell and sight of sheep carcases in full view of the children. Already she felt tainted and she wanted to shower and wash her uniform. Her mother accompanied her onto the first-year playground, which was small and neatly lawned, the building seemed quite new, it was situated a few yards away from the main school and yard, Niamh presumed this was intended to ease the new kids into high school life gently, instead of being thrown in the deep end with the big, rough, boisterous kids in the large playground.

The bell rang at 9.15 and this meant that all parents could leave the yard and let the teachers organise the new intake. They were instructed to form two lines and wait for their names to be called and placed into groups with their new teachers and new class mates. Niamh followed the group nervously to the classroom which would be where she would have to report to everyday for the next four months. Inside the class room the kids were asked to find a seat, and this would be the seat they would choose for their everyday registration in the mornings. Once seated they were each asked to introduce themselves and the new teacher would ask them a bit about where they lived or where they went for holiday in the summer, this was meant as an icebreaker and for the teacher to get some knowledge about his/her new charges. Niamh dreaded having to speak in front of stranger's, not only because she was shy but she hated the sound of her own voice because it was weak and rustic and people always commented on this when she spoke, so maybe this was the reason she wasn't assertive or confident enough to be a match for the cocky new kids that she instantly disliked. Most of them had their 'bezzy' mates from primary school with them so obviously they were all quite thick because they did not pass the exam (11 plus) to the 'winners' school. Just as she expected when Niamh spoke there were giggles about her rustic voice, she was a 'tomboy' and maybe this projected itself as she spoke. Maybe, or maybe she was a 'freak' as some scum boy pointed out to her once. That week was spent getting used to the different classrooms and different teachers for various lessons but always the same teacher for registration in the morning. Most of the teachers were cold and indifferent, the cookery teacher was horrible or maybe that was because she was still a 'Miss' into her late thirty's and probably sexually frustrated! Now, the P.E teacher was a different ball game all together, so to speak. She was a nasty piece of work. Niamh's first meeting with her was terrifying! Miss Cheery and her two 'cronies' introduced themselves to the new intake in the changing rooms next to the Gym. "Right" she said in a stern, shrieking voice, "I expect people to shut it as soon as I speak and as you get to know me you will find that I don't take any messing about, because that is when I get nasty, so you don't want to see me get nasty do you? Because that is when I get my *whip* out and start *whipping* people". WHAT! Did Niamh just imagine that? "Is she for real? Or is she joking with us?" She mortified. At this moment, the only Black girl in the group was staring at Miss C. with disbelief, Niamh couldn't believe what Miss. C. said next. "Don't you dare give me them *Black looks* lady, I am deadly serious, so do not get on the wrong side of me"!

Niamh felt sick inside and her heart was racing so fast that she was sure the three teachers would hear it and as a punishment she would be made an example of to be a warning to the other girls. That moment seemed to last forever only to be broken by Miss. C stating further that she expected every girl to have a shower after each activity and to make sure of this her or one of her cronies would be standing in the shower block to *observe.* The three cronies were made up of Miss Cheery, Miss Montrose, Mrs. Flatt and later to join the team of 'psychos' was Miss Latex. Ironically Niamh was never assaulted by Miss. C but she would later be assaulted by all the other three *twisted c****!*

That night for obvious reasons Niamh could not sleep, her parents noted that she wasn't herself at tea time around the table and she seemed to be pre-occupied with washing her hands and repeating certain manoeuvre's like taking a step back before coming to the table it was as though she had to perform these movements before she could sit down and eat her food which wasn't welcomed because her appetite was failing. Her parents were oblivious to what was happening, but Niamh knew she couldn't stop thinking of the faces of the three horrible P.E teachers who had threatened to harm her and she had to repeat her movements until she had the face of her beloved teacher from her Primary school Mrs. Welcome, in her mind, as this soothed her, and the image of the *twisted c****subsided for the time being.

# Chapter 7

# TEACHERS

The weeks past slowly, every lesson seemed like a year and Christmas seemed a century away, one lesson Niamh enjoyed was English, the teacher Mrs. Bleefully was a beautifully spoken lady and Niamh enjoyed her reading to the class, it was calming for her and seemed to take her off into a fantasy world of mystical lands and characters. The library teacher Miss. Cramp was the opposite, a horrible, bitter, twisted little woman who obviously had to be on her guard so that pupils would not ridicule her legs that were clad in irons. She suffered polio as a child and this left her a cripple, so maybe she could be forgiven for being a horrible little sod! Niamh often wondered why these people decided on a teaching career when they obviously hated kids. There again Niamh was beginning to hate the same vile kids as well.

Mr. Lobside was the History teacher and Niamh couldn't help noticing that he *never* acknowledged her even though he was her tutor in two subjects throughout her time at the school, he wasn't cruel or kind, he just did not care that she was in the room. Niamh started to realise that all Mr. L was interested in was his 'pretty boy' football team that he was the coach of. The sickly *t*\*\*\*\* who sucked up to him as much as he sucked up to them. The perfect prefect boys who were all in the top sets, no one, but no one was in the team from the low sets. This discriminating so called 'Catholic' teacher had no time for the boys or girls in the lower sets and he did not care who noticed or maybe he just thought that nobody would notice. He was a pretentious, arrogant man with an irritating upper- class accent that he constantly bragged about.

**So, not a good start for Niamh, ridiculed, ignored and friendless, it was straight down the slippery slope from now on.**

Niamh tried hard to absorb her studies, she loved the French lessons and the story books that illustrated everyday life in a French town. Her favourite subjects were English, History, Music and Art and given the right nurturing in those early days, she felt that she could have achieved in these subjects, but she wasn't nurtured, she was overlooked, not important, not a teacher's pet or a guaranteed achiever! Not one for the book of fame for the school, not a good advertisement for the school. *A Nothing!*

One of Niamh's acquaintances who had attended her primary school and had moved to the 'Losers' school with her was a loud-mouthed lowlife who's only vocabulary was 'shut ya mouth you '. Niamh had been quite friendly with Denya Yogg at primary but as soon as they transferred to high school it was as though they had never met, as was with the rest of the other four girls who had been quite friendly at primary but abandoned Niamh at high school. All through each lesson Niamh had to endure DY flirting with the boys and constantly saying "shut ya mouth you". This became mental torture for Niamh, she despised this moron and she could not concentrate on writing while this voice was repeating itself over and over and over, and surprise, surprise the teacher in charge did ***nothing.*** Niamh found herself fantasising about chocking this girl to death, it became a comfort thought of finally putting an end to that imboceale's voice and cocky ways.

***So, on many occasion Niamh found herself alone in the classroom and on the playground.***

No one wanted to be her friend and on a few occasions, she realised that she was being `used' by certain girls who's best friend might have been off ill and needed someone to stand next to in the dinner que or on the cold, depressing play ground that day, but as soon as the best friend returned to school Niamh was dropped like a vat of acid. Friday afternoons were a welcomed time, the last lesson was always P.E and cross country. Niamh did her fastest to get around the course and back to have a shower in private, change into her uniform ready for the 3.30 home time bell. The run started off ok but soon the smell of the dead sheep from the abattoir would consume her nostrils and violate her mind, the sight of the carcases piled up on top of one another was traumatic for her, she loved all animals and she had never encountered how they were slaughtered or where this took place, but here on this P.E activity every Friday afternoon she was subjected to this ***misery.*** There was no way around it, the track ran a long side the railway line and the girls were forbidden to step onto the track for fear of electric shock, "never mind" she thought to herself "I will soon be home and I can get straight into the shower and wash off the stench from this vile place, and my mother will put my uniform into the washing machine and it will be cleansed of this filth".

# Chapter 8

# WEEKEND

Friday tea time was magical for Niamh, she was freed from that vile place and had two whole days at home with her family and pets, as soon as she came through her front door off came the uniform and straight into the shower, the warm comfort of the water and the smell of imperial leather soap was heaven, but first she had to gather her uniform and place it in a plastic carrier bag so that it could not contaminate her when she came out of the shower all disinfected and cleansed from *evil*. She would inform her mother where the clothing was so that she would not be searching for it when it came to wash day on the Saturday. In the shower, Niamh had scrubbed every inch of her anatomy over and repeatedly," maybe one more time "she said to herself "and then I will get out and dry myself and put my PJs on and relax downstairs watching TV". "Ok, one more time, nearly there, one last time, well maybe another scrub for good measure", this went on and on for the best part of an hour. "What are you doing Niamh? "her mother shouts curiously. "Tea time". "Ok," said Niamh "enough is enough" and leaves the shower, dries off, talc and deodorant then PJs on, mission accomplished, just then her mother is standing there with the carrier bag of Niamh`s uniform inside, takes out the clothing to place in the laundry basket and as doing so the clothes brush the arm of Niamh and disaster strikes. "No" she shrieks "What are you doing that for? It's taken me ages to get clean and now you have made me dirty again". Her mother stairs at her in confusion, not having a clue what she is shouting about. Niamh turns and darts back into the shower to repeat the cleansing ritual again for another thirty minutes.

This time she is cautious and makes sure that her mother and the tainted school uniform are nowhere in sight, she finally makes it down the stairs into the lounge and snuggles up on the couch. After tea, which she struggles to finish because of the trauma of the day, Niamh and her family settle down to watch the Friday night movie on TV. Struggling to keep her eyes open she is determined to make every hour of her weekend last for ever.

Home work was a trial because she couldn't bear to look at or touch the contaminated books from that vile school when she was in the sanctuary of her home, so gradually she got behind with her work. A few weeks later Niamh would experience ***physical abuse*** at the hands of the 'golden girl' of her class. Jolene Deed was the leader of the 'klick' of girls whom had come to high school together from their primary school somewhere in Mungchester unlike the girls who came to high school with Niamh from her little village in the country they all stuck together and JD was the ring leader, she was the glamour girl of the class, perfect shiny, long hair, immaculately turned out, but she was a nasty, spoilt little *b*\*\*\*\* and Niamh despised her, even more so after this incident in English class one Friday afternoon. Last lesson ... As usual Niamh was sat on her own at a desk meant for two- people, everyone had their 'bezzy' mates sat next to them but Niamh was alone, she was getting used to this and just accepted the fact that she must be a '*freak*' and that is why nobody wanted to speak to her or worse sit next to her, she didn't have B.O or head lice, on the contrary she was well dressed and cleaner than anyone because of her cleaning rituals that could last an hour easily. So, what was it? What was the reason that she couldn't make new friends or that anyone wanted to be her 'bessy' mate, even the *c*\*\*\*\* that she knew from primary didn't want to no her anymore, they seemed to have made new friends also. Was it the fact that she had curly black hair and not the long blonde hair of most other girls with the perfect flick back parting and blue eyes, her skin was dark, and her eyes were dark, maybe this was the cause of the delusion that she wasn't white but black.

So, back to the '*assault*', half way through the lesson Miss Piece was getting more and more annoyed at JD for constantly chatting away to her sickly side kick Alison Laslaw, another bitch with perfect hair and blue eyes who was always brushing the thing during lesson time *strange!* Finally, Miss P. snapped and demanded that JD go and sit next to Niamh so she would stop chatting and get on with some work, how *cruel* of the teacher to do this to Niamh, she knew that Niamh never spoke and so she used her to punish JD by not having anyone to natter to. Suddenly JD went into a rage and refused to move, only on the threat of the headmistress made JD jump up, grab her bag and books and reluctantly move towards Niamh, the whole class watched in silence as JD screamed at the teacher, "I hate her she never speaks" and as she shouted this out she rammed the chair into Niamh's chair and hurt Niamh's leg in the process. It was the *humiliation* that hurt the most, the injured leg was a reminder of how much she was hated by these people. Niamh could feel her face burn with embarrassment and she wanted to curl up and hide somewhere. JD edged as far away from Niamh as she could, she looked like she was hanging off the edge of a cliff rather than go overboard to certain death. The incompetent teacher just looked on and never even asked Niamh if she was ok or worse still she didn't have the decency to save Niamh from this humiliation and move the piece of *s\*\*\** away from her. *WHY?* The home time bell rang out and Niamh sighed with huge relief to get away from the horrible incident with JD and she just wanted to get home. JD practically jumped out of her seat as though she was running away from a person with leprosy and she immediately launched into rapid conversation about her ordeal having to sit next to the *'Freak'!* As usual, Niamh was the first through the door, down to the coat room and up into the town centre to get her bus, she was afraid of reprisals from JD and her many scum mates for the inconvenience that was bestowed on JD by the heartless teacher forcing her to sit next to Niamh for the lesson. The route to the town centre included crossing the bridge over the railway track, this area of ground was the place where you would be expected to have a fight with whoever you had 'upset' during the day and a gang would gather at the first rumour of a fight, the perpetrator would wait menacingly on the bridge for the intended target and immediately launch into an attack.

**So, the sooner you were over that bridge the better chance you had of staying safe.**

Niamh sometimes wondered if any other pupil was having the same traumatic experience of high school as she was and time and time again she would study people around her to possibly catch an incident but no, she never did see anybody else get 'picked on' as she did. There were occasional fights in the playground but there was always a reason behind it i.e. football disputes, pushing in at the ice cream van que but never anything that had happened to herself for no reason at all. She started to believe her own press that she was a freak and a magnet for bullies.

# Chapter 9

# THE MIRROR

Once safe on the bus Niamh could relax but her mind was running wild, she couldn't wait to get home and get into the shower and put her uniform in the washing machine. She couldn't stop thinking of JD and how she despised her, she fantasised about torturing her to death slowly. That night after an hour in the bathroom, constantly washing the contamination away Niamh settled down with her family to watch TV. All to soon the evening came to an end and her parents said it was time for bed, so Niamh and her sister had supper and went upstairs past the mirror hanging in the hallway at the foot of the stairs, suddenly as Niamh glanced into the mirror the image of JD appeared, she glanced again to rectify it with an image of her best friend DF who she was separated from, but the face of JD was still present in the reflection and would not go away. Niamh felt that she could not pass the mirror without rectifying the fault in the reflection because if she didn't then something bad may happen to her family, she needed to keep them safe, she needed to keep evil out of her home, so she concentrated long and hard until the reflection was a friend and not an enemy, exhausted she fell into bed and fast asleep.

Christmas was approaching and so were the tests (S.A.T.S) to determine who stays in their sets or who goes down to lower sets or up to higher sets. **A** was the top pupil's domain and **E** was where the pupils who were not expected to make anything of their lives, but as Niamh found the low groups were the '*salt of the earth*' kids and they were kind and good fun and never said a wrong word to her, unlike the top kids who were vile and Niamh hated them with passion.

By now Niamh`s mental health was failing fast and furious and revision wasn`t an option, in her fragile mind the whole school, teacher`s, pupils even the actual building and its location were taking over her thoughts day and night. She had her hate list building up of the people who had threatened her and the fact that she didn`t have a loyal friend to fall back on or anyone to talk to, she had to deal with the torment all alone. She was far too busy battling her demons to even care about revising, she just couldn`t cope with both, at the back of her mind she wanted to please her parents and do well academically but it was impossible. The situation was going to get much worse before it got better. The week of the exams. Niamh just stared at the exam papers, she hadn't a clue about what the questions were asking her or what the answers should be because for the last four months she had been withdrawing into her own little world of rituals to keep her family safe. So, she babbled through the exams and wrote down anything in terrible, scruffy handwriting that used to be so beautiful when she was at her primary school, she also had to keep writing over the same word as part of her ritual, for example if she wrote a word but had the image of either JD or the three '*sick c\*\*\*\**' the PE teachers, then she would have to re write the word until she could only see people that she liked in her mind, only then could she move onto the next word, so you can see how this craziness prevented Niamh from ever succeeding academically!

The following week was results week and in a very cruel fashion each teacher would read out to the whole class each person's result in order of where they came in the class i.e. 1$^{st}$, 2$^{nd}$ and very last, yes that's right Niamh was the very last with the least marks in every subject. But the worse was her Maths test … **6** out of a **100**! What kind of cruel *B******* would do that to an 11-year-old girl who was suffering from a mental disorder! Even though Mr.Conk had no idea of what Niamh was going through, she couldn't believe that he would be so cruel surely this was a breach of confidentiality**!** How dare he share her results with the whole class and subject her to ridicule**!**

After ten minutes the class settled down again, they had laughed at Niamh and taunted her about being a thick sod and stating that she was on her way down to the lower-class group **B**!

This treatment lasted a whole week with each class teacher reading out results, the class and Niamh knew that she was the class 'Dunce'.

That night around the dinner table, once again Niamh was quiet and subdued, when asked if anything was wrong by her parents she would answer the same, that she was just tired, when really, she wanted to cry out loud. After dinner the usual ritual, into the shower to scrub the contamination of the day away, bed time past the mirror in the hall and the battle starts, this time it was the whole class and the teachers who had ridiculed her all week, this was exhausting, the list of demons were growing and more demons meant more mental fight back and more rituals, she had to stop the images of the scum she hated from appearing in the reflection and wait until she could see nice people like a famous person. A favourite vision was of the 'Avengers' Joanna Lumley and Gareth Hunt who were Niamh's mental defenders for the next decade, these celebs were her own little army of heroes who would avenge her in her mind. She would enlist them as her weapons and fight against evil. She collected pictures from newspapers and hid them around her bedroom as though it was a shrine to her favourite allies, she felt safe with them and wrote their names around the place and hidden in her school bag. They were her version of garlic to vampires but these vampires were the teachers and pupils of St. Gonner's High School.

Many time's Niamh would look at the coat of arms of the school that was on every uniform and hung over the school entrance, it basically stood for faith, love, and learning and as Niamh thought to herself "what a load of s\*\*\*"! So, the delusions were well established in Niamh's mind and so was her coping method or 'protection' as she preferred to think of it as, she had her strategies put in place, this made things easier to deal with but no less exhausting.

At last the Christmas holidays were here and nothing else mattered to Niamh but the next two whole weeks at home with her family and the magic of Christmas. Even though she knew deep down that there was no Father Christmas, but at the age of 12 she still pretended he was real and asked her parents to still hide her and her sisters presents. Niamh had always loved Christmas and hated January because it was so depressing and such an anti-climax from the last few weeks, and when all the decorations had to come down, well, it was as though the world had ended for Niamh, but this year would be much worse because she had to return to the 'vile place' on the 1st of January 1976.

# Chapter 10

# **GOING DOWN**

Monday morning, standing at a cold, wet bus stop on a miserable, grey ` after Christmas blues' day at 8am, horrible.

Niamh knew that she was going down to B group, she wondered if the group would be friendly to her or ignore her as the A group had done, she tried to be optimistic but deep down her premonition told her that nothing would be different and, yes, she was right.

The form teacher was the same cold, heartless *b*\*\*\*\* who insisted that the scum JD sit next to Niamh last term to stop her from talking during class lesson. Miss P. was a weak, meek and nervous person who couldn't really command respect from an insulant pupil, maybe this was why she appeared `inhuman' maybe she couldn't afford to show any familiarity, she would often threaten with sending the offender to the two `pastoral' care teachers. Mrs Plaint for the girls and Mr. Farthing for the boys and knowing these two-evil *b*\*\*\*\*\*\*\* as Niamh did the threat always worked.

So, Miss P. read out the registration list and never even mentioned or welcomed any new comers to the group, the first thing that irritated Niamh was that three of the boys answered their names to numbers of the football teams of the time, how cocky and thick she thought but these three boys were to be the most hated by Niamh, especially one of them Donald Croaks, he would be the second person to assault Niamh after J.D with the desk chair. Niamh sensed that this boy disliked her but as usual she had no idea why. One day after the dinner time bell rang, Niamh made her way down the stairs towards the dinner hall, suddenly she felt a thud to her side, at first she thought someone had accidentally bumped into her and she was expecting an apology but she couldn't have been more wrong, there at the bottom of the stairs was D.C, a small, scruffy boy with untidy blonde hair and beady, rat like eyes he confronted Niamh with another thump on her arm, threatening to fight her because he made the excuse that she had bumped into him on the stairs. Everyone around could see that this was clearly an excuse for D.C to physically assault Niamh, they must have been in on it because not one said or did anything to protect her, it was only the appearance of the teacher on the stairs that defused the situation. Niamh was shaken and she felt sick and wanted to cry but she gathered her strength in the comfort that she would use all her mental power to put a curse on this boy and so every day when D.C was ever late for school, which he often was, she would pray that he had been killed crossing the road. It never happened but it was a coping strategy for Niamh and she learned to live with the disappointment that he was never crippled under the wheels of a car.

The other two boys were not as bad, but they did ridicule Niamh`s name and the way she spoke, which wasn't very often, they would throw pencils at her and pretend it wasn't them but D.C openly harassed her, he was hell bent on finding any excuse to attack Niamh. The sad thing is that if she had told her father of this, he would have totally obliterated these 'thugs 'and he would have proudly gone to prison for the privilege. Niamh knew this, but she didn't want her father to be taken away from the family home or her mother be upset, so as usual she kept quiet.

All this bullying only fuelled the belief that Niamh was a 'freak' especially after she had been called that on a few occasions. Niamh hated B group and the people in it, they were more horrible than A group she did her best to avoid confrontation and kept her head down as if this was a way of survival in a shark infested sea.

So, Maths class with new maths teacher the horrible Mrs. Plaint, she was a cruel woman who relished in her role as 'top dog' amongst the girls in the school, any threat of being 'sent' to her for chastising would result in fear and tears from even the hardest low life in the school. So, it gradually became obvious to Mrs. P that Niamh was 'thick' at Maths, which, yes, she was. On top of her personal turbulence Niamh was calcaemic but if she had the right mentoring and support she felt she could have conquered this. Mrs. P never concerned herself with Niamh until she teamed up with the *b\*\*\*\*\*\** Mr. Farthing, he was the male equivalent to Mrs. P, and for some reason he disliked Niamh immensely, she was in his Geography lesson and he never spoke to her or offered help or support or even tried to find out the reason that she wasn't doing her homework or that her writing was atrocious. Maybe it was the fact that Niamh didn't flirt with him or fancy him as other girls did in the school, the rumour was that Mr. F would stop at your bus stop in the morning to offer you a lift, only if you were pretty and had a huge bust, it didn't matter if it was a hurricane brewing, if you were ugly he would drive straight past. Anyway, that would be a different story! So, Mr. F had started to complain about Niamh to Mrs. P who was determine to 'sort her out'.

This partnership turned into an obsession for both teachers, they had teamed up to 'bully' Niamh for whatever problem they had with her. Niamh felt that Mr. F was the cause of it, she felt that he disliked her immensely and as punishment decided to make her school life difficult by having Mrs. P put the fear of 'Hitler' into her. He later told her parents at parents evening that Niamh was insolent towards him and would not take instructions or do any work in his class. Niamh's mother pointed out to him that Niamh did not like him and he said the feeling was mutual, so, there you have it. So, these two horrible beings kept an evil eye on Niamh they were picking at everything they could to make her feel intimidated. Strange that Mr. F was so concerned about Niamh's school work but he never spoke to her in class. Very Strange!

By now Niamh's rituals at home were spiralling out of control, the constant washing in the shower, the hand scrubbing, the nightly rituals when all her family were fast asleep, poor Niamh was standing in front of the mirror in the hall trying to exorcize the demons looking back at her. The trick was to keep focused on her reflection until she could see someone she liked or one of her celebrity heroes like Joanna Lumley, instead of the vile scum whom she despised from school, the list was growing and now there were several faces taunting her in the mirror, the vile boys in her form, the two teachers Mr. F and Mrs. P, and as always, the first person to assault her at high school, J.D. So, this could take up to two or three hours and sometimes all night, how could a 12-year-old girl possibly concentrate on her school work with all this going on in her head. One-night Niamh's mother awoke to go to the bathroom and that is when she found Niamh sitting on the stairs crying, she was exhausted and although she was upset at her mother seeing her crying, she was mega relieved that she could finally tell her parents what was going on. For some time, they could see that Niamh was acting strange, but they thought it would pass or that it was maybe teenage hormones, in fact they weren't quite sure what was causing these 'silly' rituals. Niamh cried and cried as her mother cradled her and assured her that her and dad would get to the bottom of this and sort it out. Niamh was taken into bed with her parents, comforted and soothed into a good night's sleep.

*The next day Niamh was kept off school and taken to the Doctors were an appointment to see a child psychologist was put in place.*

# Chapter 11

# THE SICK NOTE

Niamh was allowed off school for the rest of the week because her mother could see how drained she was, and she was very worried about her even though she kept her concern hidden from Niamh. The new week and Niamh was back at school, her mother told her that she would ring the school and explain why she had been absent. Whilst in a lesson, a message was delivered to the class teacher that Mrs. P wished to speak with Niamh regarding her absence the following week, so, at break time Niamh went along to the staff room and asked for Mrs. P.

As soon as she saw Niamh she immediately said, "sick note, where is it?" She didn't ask if Niamh was better, she didn't even say hello to her, she was the inhuman beast that Niamh always thought she was. "I don't have one, my mother is phoning the school office today" replied Niamh, suddenly without a word Mrs. P produced a huge bamboo cane and demanded Niamh hold her hand out, Niamh was afraid and she couldn't believe what was happening this was being carried out in front of other pupils and staff walking past the staff room in the communal hall. Thrash, thrash rite across Niamh`s wrist, brusing her vain and stinging her bones. "Insolence" was all Mrs. P could say and threatened another assault if she didn't produce a sick note the next day. Mrs. P didn't even give Niamh the chance to finish her sentence about her mother contacting the office, she was delighted at the chance of striking this girl that herself and Mr. F had taken such a dislike to. Later that day Mrs. P took great delight in ringing Niamh's mother and telling her that her beloved daughter had had to be caned due to her being insolent to her when asked for a sick note. For a few seconds Mrs. P was in her glory until Niamh's mother keeping her dignity, pointed out her disgust and anger at what Mrs. P had just done because Niamh was mentally ill and was been treated by a child psychologist. Well, you can imagine the panic the evil *c*\*\*\*\* must have gone into, her job could be at steak if an investigation was to take place. So, the evil Mrs. P did a complete 'turnaround' towards Niamh, she went into 'overdrive' in a bid to keep her job and career and avoid being sued for assaulting a mentally ill 12-year-old, fragile little girl! She would offer Niamh a half hour extra tuition every morning and she even drove Niamh home at home time. This 'kindness was short lived when Mrs. P was satisfied that she was not going to be investigated by police or be sued by Niamh's parents. Niamh would have preferred Mrs. P to be burnt at the stake but unfortunately that would only happen in one of her 'revenge 'fantasies when she was alone at night in her bed. Mr. F was unapologetic or unsympathetic towards Niamh or the fact that he had wound up Mrs. P to bully Niamh. Mr. F. fancied himself as a lady's man. He also fancied himself as a hard man. Niamh often thought to herself how her father would put Mr. F in his place with one swift 'left hook' and her father would have if only Niamh told him, but fear of her father going to prison put a stop to this notion. To this day, Niamh never knew just what this *b*\*\*\*\*\*\* had against her. It was early in the term that Niamh witnessed Mr. F threatening to throw a 'gobby' girl through a 2nd floor window outside his classroom, the girl was younger than Niamh and was clearly upset about something, and wanted her best friend to comfort her. It turns out that this girl called Anne was in a separate lesson to Niamh when her teacher had made an arrogant remark about her home life. "You only come to school for a roof over your head "was the remark from the offending teacher so the rumour was, the poor girl was so humiliated in front of a laughing class that all she could do was to run out of the room and find her best friend who was in Mr. Fs lesson. Niamh admired this girl because she stood up to this six foot bully who was meant to be a 'pastoral care 'supervisor, what a joke! Niamh could see in Mr. Fs face that he would have loved nothing more than to carry out his threat of throwing the girl through the nearest window but he eventually backed down when the girl called his bluff. Good for you, Niamh thought to herself.

# Chapter 12

# NETBALL

Wednesday was always a welcome day for Niamh because it was half way through to wonderful Friday. Poor Niamh was just wishing her young life away, at a time when she should have been at her happiest. She should have been going to teenage parties, wearing make-up and dating boys, but apart from the fact that she was never asked and totally ignored by other teenagers around her, she just wasn't switched on to the transition from child to adult. It just wasn't there because she was mentally ill and far too busy dealing with her obsessional delusions and pure hatred of the people around her who she blamed for not being normal. Wednesday was also P.E day, the dreaded three, twisted *c*\*\*\*\* would be on duty, ready to assault any girl who dared to disobey them. Still, at least it wasn't 'cross country', that was on a Friday. No, Wednesday was basketball in the gym. Niamh quite enjoyed the game but again she didn't follow it up as a hobby or join the school team because of her hatred of the vile place, teachers and pupils, so again Niamh was stumped! The lesson was under way and for once Niamh seemed slightly enthusiastic and tried to become a team player, she was trying her best when suddenly the whistle blew! Niamh was laughing at something that one of the nicer girls had said to her about something trivial, when all of a sudden the twisted *c*\*\*\* of a P.E teacher Miss Latex screamed in a rage about girls still talking after she had blown the whistle and instantly looked at Niamh, "come here" she shouted, "come here now", at first Niamh thought that Miss. L was Looking straight past her at someone else but no, she was looking at Niamh. In disbelief once again Niamh slowly walked towards the twisted *b\*\*\*\** and stood there in silence while Miss. L waited for a few seconds as though to let Niamh stew for a minute as a warning, the few seconds seemed like a whole hour, what was she doing? Why was she staring at Niamh in silence? Suddenly Miss. L said abruptly "No, I will have to discipline you, bend over". Whack, whack again, across Niamh`s bottom this time. Niamh was in shock again, but in a sadistic way she wasn't shocked because she had kind of accepted that this treatment of her was going to keep happening again and again and again, in fact if there was a day that passed without any form of abuse towards her, whether it be slight or heavy then she would worry more at night because she thought the abuse was being kept back to a build-up of something huge! Was this all imagined? What was happening to her? Her mind was spiralling out of control, she was enraged with hate and revenge! It was just short of a miracle that she didn't go into a rage and kill this *f\*\*\*\*\*\** piece of *s\*\*\** there and then, if she could only make herself invisible and strangle this sick, twisted, arrogant, power crazy, self- obsessed *f\*\*\** with the chain that held the whistle around her neck then laugh as she struggled and turned blue. "How *f\*\*\*\*\*\** dare you, how *f\*\*\*\*\*\**dare you hit me, who do you think you are, you are a *f\*\*\*\*\*\** piece of dirt, I hope you die in agony then rot in hell!

Niamh woke up in a sweat, she had been fantasising that much before she fell asleep that the fantasies carried on into

her dream, she was so traumatised at the beating she had
been handed out from the P.E teacher Miss. Latex during
Net ball practise that day that she spent all night imagining
what she would do to the bitch for revenge. The frustration
was crippling because Niamh didn't posess special powers
or she didn't have an invisible suit to enable her to creep up
on the witch after school just as she was getting into her car
and slit her throat.

### *This was to be Niamh`s 4th physical assault at this`*
### *vile place'.*

By now it was becoming clear to other pupils that
Niamh was a bit of a `push over' and one tiny little squirt
of a girl tried to assert her power over Niamh by purposely
dropping her pen onto the floor and telling Niamh to pick
it up. This cocky `thing' was called Kirsty Neuter and she
was the cousin of J.D the brat who assaulted Niamh with
a chair for having to sit next to her. So, little Kirsty`s desk
was situated behind Niamh`s desk in the registration class,
one day as Niamh sat quietly waiting to answer to her name
that she was in attendance, she heard a voice behind her
saying "eh, eh Conlen" at first Niamh ignored the `dwarf
'she felt insulted that this little nothing was addressing her
by her last name, how low life, how rough, how cocky,
how dare she. Niamh turned around to see what this girl
wanted because she was embarrassed and wanted the girl to
stop calling her by her last name. "What" she said defiantly
and surprisingly, she had developed an inner strength when
pushed to the limit. The `dwarf' laughed and pointed to
her pen on the floor, then turning to her friend sat next to

her, she had an audience, she looked right at Niamh and said "pick that up", "no" said Niamh even under the threat of reprisals from the dwarf`s many cousins at the school, Niamh knew there was no way she could give in to this demand or her life would be made even more miserable at school than it already was.

*Maybe if Niamh had one big fight with someone, she might have gained respect, but she had been brought up decent, her mother always taught her to be `lady like at all times'!*

# Chapter 13

# THE RULER

Miss Molotoff was a small, stocky, woman, a well-toned physique with fiery red hair and a sharp Irish accent that could cut you to the bone with one word. She never smiled but powted she never laughed but shouted. She was relatively attractive and she knew it, she loved nothing more than to strut her arrogant stuff along the corridor and god help any pupil who didn't move out of her way on a busy corridor, she never stepped aside for anyone, except the headmaster, maybe! Niamh was under the care of Miss. M for three sessions a week twice for P.E and once for R.E, but Niamh always wondered why Miss. M was preaching Religion, seeing as she was a horrible soul! She would sit at her desk as though she didn't want to be there, it was clear that she would much rather be in the gym showing off her trampoline skills or her netball moves than stuck inside with a bunch of annoying kids.

It was a depressing Monday afternoon and it was also R.E. The class was set work to do by Miss. M, everything was running smoothly just as she liked it, until a messenger knocked on the door before being asked to "enter". Miss. M was wanted in the office, a telephone call was waiting for her. "Right" she said, "I must go to the office to take this phone call but that doesn't mean that you can talk, if I find anyone talking when I return they will be in deep trouble, do you understand me?"

As expected everybody in the room answered, "yes miss" in a sickly, 'sucking up to teacher' way. So, the minute Miss. M had left the room the whole class burst into conversation, yes everybody except Niamh. Apart from the fact that Niamh would be too scared to speak when told not to do, but nobody ever spoke to her. So, Niamh could honestly say to herself that she had been the victim of injustice again. Ten minutes' past before Miss. M came bursting through the class room door to an unruly class of 'chatterboxes'. Seething with temper and rage, she snapped "who was speaking?" as she did so her lips became pinched and blue, trying to compose herself she said" Right, seeing as no one wants to own up to disobeying my orders, I will punish you all, roll up your sleeves". Moving up and down each isle of desk seats Miss. M assaulted each pupil with a thick long ruler that she kept next to the blackboard.

### *So, now we are onto Niamh's 5ᵗʰ assault at High school.*

At home Niamh's behaviour is out of control, she couldn't move without having to repeat the same movement over and over. She had developed a strategy for getting passed the mirror in the hall easier, it consisted of using a small mirror that was in the bird cage in the lounge. The idea came to her suddenly one night as she was watching the two budgies playing with their mirror. She said to herself" look how the birds, love mirrors and I hate them", but then a voice spoke to her in her head and said" why don't you borrow their mirror, if you can`t get passed the hall mirror then take the budgie mirror with you ". This enabled Niamh to transport the evil visions that she saw in the hall mirror, upstairs with her to her bedroom, where she could concentrate under the covers by torchlight and put negatives to positives by constant staring in the mirror until she could see the face of Joanna Lumley, her hero and if she could keep that thought there for at least a couple of minutes then the whole thing was made safe. This is very` looney' behaviour to the normal person but in Niamh's mind it was the only way to go about her life and the reason it was all done for … to keep her family safe.

# Chapter 14

# BLOOD INVASION

Niamh was from a musical family and she loved playing records at home, she loved hearing her mother playing the piano at weekends when she had some free time, so the music lesson at school was welcomed, it was a relief to close her eyes as instructed by the teacher and listen to classical music, it was soothing to her. One day another` goby' girl was forced to sit next to Niamh to stop her from chatting to her `mate 'and make her concentrate. Niamh didn't dislike this girl it was just that the girl was a friend of the hated J.D and Niamh felt this girl was contaminated due to that fact alone. As she sat next to Niamh she began to show her how she had cut her finger the day before on some glass that she accidentally broke. Niamh looked at the finger, it looked very sore and she just said, "that looks bad" "yes" said the girl "it is", at that moment the girl caught her finger under the desk lid and it started to bleed. To someone else this would be something that they wouldn't give a second thought to, but for Niamh it was making her un easy, she didn't want to be contaminated by the blood of a friend of J. Ds whom Niamh despised with every breath in her body. Suddenly, the bell rang and just as Niamh predicted to herself the bleeding finger collided with her sleeve, her blazer sleeve. The girl had unwittingly brushed her finger against Niamh and there was the tiniest smear of blood on Niamh`s jacket. First, she felt sick, then she went into an inner panic,

52

then she felt anger and she kept questioning why? Why has this happened to her? Why has the blood of this person been put into her, you see in Niamh's poorly, tormented mind this smudging of blood had entered her blood stream, crazy as it seems but that is how it was. No matter how many times she scrubbed herself with a scrubbing brush that night in the shower she could never get that streak of blood out of her bloodstream. This idea went on for a couple of years the reasoning behind it was total delusion. Niamh firmly believed that the girls blood had somehow travelled through her clothing and entered her veins, this was torture for Niamh sometimes she would forget about it and allow herself to be in a good mood, but when she remembered the situation she would break out in a cold sweat, she felt desperate that she couldn't confide in anyone.

*The vile place had finally claimed Niamh by inserting blood into her body from someone who was from the school and town that she despised, this would be the very first time that Niamh found herself asking why was she alive? Why was she enduring all this horribleness? Why wasn't the scum from the school suffering like she was? What was wrong with her? She just wanted to be normal!*

# Chapter 15

# ABBA

School day mornings for Niamh were always greeted with Radio 2 music, hosted by the brilliant Terry Wogan. God rest his soul. His wonderful manner and cheerfulness were a blessing in the mornings, he always made Niamh feel that there was a nicer world out there instead of school, and when she is 16 she will hopefully find it. He made life seem fun with his calming, Irish accent and positive outlook on everything. So, Niamh knew every song that he would play between 7.00 am and 8.15 am every week day. One song that kept popping up was a catchy feel good number that Niamh couldn't get out of her head. Who were these people singing on the Terry Wogan show? Where do they come from? Every single morning this song would be played by Terry, sometimes repeated on the radio in the car when Niamh`s father drove her to school. The week past and everybody was talking about this new pop group with their hit song *Dancing Queen*. Such a genius song, as Niamh always referred to a good tune. Niamh did her investigating and found the name and country of these people with the great song to be the fantastic ABBA! Niamh had requested that her parents buy her the record *Dancing Queen*. So, Christmas 1976 she received in her pile of presents the album *ABBA- ARRIVAL,* which contained the hypnotic *Dancing Queen* as well as several other equally hypnotic songs that just melted Niamh away into a world of snow-capped mountains, forests and seas. A musical, mystical fantasy of great music.

Slowly, but surely Niamh would find a beautiful escape into the world of Abba songs, she eventually knew each song word for word and note for note. She collected every album they made, these four people and their brilliant music became Niamh's 'Religion' for the rest of her life. So, you can imagine how she looked after her records and music cassettes of the super group. There was no way that her school uniform had to meet her precious Abba, to her, Abba were pure, and her uniform was evil because it represented the 'vile place' and it was contaminated! So, every Friday night after she had showered and scrubbed her body for an hour and finger nails disinfected, Niamh would carefully take out her Abba record and play it in her bedroom, she never played her music during the week because she felt that she would contaminate her beloved Abba if she touched the disks on a school day, so it had to be on a weekend only.

The Author realises that this seems crazy to the reader, and yes it was craziness for the people looking in from the outside, but Niamh didn't realise how much damage she was doing to herself because this was real to her and the only way forward.

Each Abba song had its own fantasy for Niamh, she imagined a world where everyone had luscious blonde hair and deep blue eyes, and one of her favourites was a song called *Eagle* this song was about freedom, being stunning and majestic, and having the gift to fly far away over beautiful countries, looking down on all creation. Niamh thought to herself how she would like any future boyfriends to look like the boys in Abba, so she scrutinized every blonde boy she set eyes on, this became an obsession even though no boys were interested in her at that time, Niamh knew this and never had any expectations of finding a nice boyfriend with blonde hair and blue eyes. As the obsession with Abba grew so did Niamh`s hatred of herself and this was because she had curly, jet black hair and dark eyes. She didn't want to be dark she wanted to be like the people in Abba, because blonde hair and blue eyes meant that you lived in a beautiful country and everybody fancied you. Because she was so dark this caused another painful embarrassment for Niamh, she was covered in body hair, yes, body hair and she despised every single strand of it, if she could, she would have bleached her body to kill the hair growth, but that would cause despair for her parents, so she had to live with it. One day in a history lesson, the teacher was discussing the Vikings and the Romans, Niamh was staring at her hands and wrists, she regularly looked at her hands and arms to visually despise the hair growth but something else suddenly occurred to her, she was black! "No, I'm not black", her heart was racing, she came out in a cold sweat as though she was a rabbit caught in the head lights, she tried to get away from what had just dawned on her.

Niamh didn't know what 'Racism' was and there was never any mention that she disliked people of a different colour, no, she just wanted to be blonde with blue eyes.

That night at tea time, Niamh confronted her mother about her being black, "but we aren't black, what are you talking about?" replied Kaitlyn. Niamh resented her parents for giving birth to her so dark when they knew that she wanted to be blonde with blue eyes, but they had no idea that this had become another obsession for Niamh.

Niamh's mother Kaitlyn was born with jet black hair and very dark skin, but she had blue eyes this DNA came from the family ancestry of Italian, Spanish, and French, all mixed up with Irish blood.

Niamh wasn't having any of it and the resentment grew and grew and she became argumentative and aggressive to her parents, she couldn't bear to look at them because they weren't blonde, blue eyed Vikings. Even a picture of her father as a young boy with dark blonde hair couldn't console her, she was never going to be like Abba.

# Chapter 16

# SUMMER

---

Summer holidays 1976, the weather was so hot that it was cracking the earth, the kids would cook eggs on the pavements just to see if they could. Niamh loved the hot weather, the long hot summer days of camping, playing in the woods, tree climbing, strolling down to the chippy nearby with other kids on the street for supper, under the watchful eye of her three German Shepherd dogs. At that time in history the 'Jack the Ripper' maniac was still at large in the nearby county so Niamh's parents insisted that she take the dogs everywhere with her when out playing and that's what she did. Behind Niamh's house was a building site and all the kids in the area would play on it, climbing the scaffolds, playing in the dumper truck, even after parents had warned them of the dangers, they didn't listen as kids don't. So, the glorious days of childhood school holidays should be idyllic but what if it takes you ages to get out of the house in the morning.

***This summer would be the worst in Niamh's long battle with herself and her demons.***

9 am and friends are already knocking on Niamh's door, the friends that had always been true to her but sadly did not attend the same high school as herself or things may have been different. Niamh would be exhausted after

a night of performing rituals on the stair case and battling with the demon mirror. Sometimes it would be dawn when she would finally fall into bed or fall asleep on the stairs.

"Come on you two, everyone is waiting to play out and the dogs are all excited and ready to go" shouted Niamh`s mother. "Come and get your breakfasts, get washed and dressed for the day". Niamh`s sister Lizzy would be up and out as soon as she had her breakfast. Lizzy was a different `kettle of fish' to Niamh, she was totally normal, and life was a joy for her, she enjoyed every day and never had a day of `blues 'ever. Niamh wondered on many occasion what was the difference in her and her sister, they were both from the same gene- pool but one was afflicted and one was happy.

"Come on Niamh" were the shouts from her sister and friends, "we are making a secret `den' in the woods". Niamh`s heart sank as she attempted to get dressed for the day, clothes on negative thought, clothes off, try again, clothes on and off and on and so on and so on. The more she struggled under pressure, the stronger the demons became, and they kept on dragging her back to her rituals. An hour would pass easily, and Niamh was just on the verge of going through the front door, finally she was through, but the rituals didn't stop there, once past the front door she had to battle the garden path and gate, one step forward and ten steps back.

Late afternoon and Niamh was out playing with friends, for a time she was content, she soaked up the sunshine and adored the smell of the woods and fields but soon it would be tea time and she would have to go through the whole routine again before she could get out to play after her meal. Sometimes she would just abandon the idea and stay in and watch T.V.

Another coping strategy Niamh invented for herself was the 'sort it out later' approach. For example, if she was attempting to go out to play with friends as in the latter, and her mother or father were getting inpatient with her, she would put this into play and it seemed to work for her. She referred to this as 'securing' her routine to have a safe, positive day, it meant that the demons would allow Niamh to carry out her rituals in the evening and that would cancel out any bad luck or negative vibes from the day and so, the day would be unruined. It was as though the demons were debt collectors and if she paid up sometime during that day then no further action would be taken for while at least.

**By now, Niamh had learned the rules of her torment, if she did not obey the demons, they would make her suffer.**

# Chapter 17

# THE TENT

Niamh`s very best estranged friend Delia Fawcett was coming to stay for the weekend, it was some time since they had seen each other so they had a lot of catching up to do. Someone suggested that they camp out in the garden tents for the night, that would be fun she thought so that is what they did. Niamh was so excited, it was going to be a good night, so after supper the little group of friends settled into two tents pitched up by her father in Niamh`s back garden. They used torches to see each other and they laughed and told scary stories while cuddling up to the dogs for warmth and comfort. Everything was going fine and dandy until disaster struck! Niamh was joking about and making shapes from her own shadow by torchlight, she suddenly stopped in her tracks and said "no, go away, don't you dare spoil my fun", poor Niamh had seen the silhouette of a horrible person from the `vile place' in her shadow, she kept trying to get her own silhouette back, but she just couldn't do it. She just went silent as she tried frantically to `sort it out'. D.F wasn't amused, she was baffled and insulted why Niamh had suddenly changed into a dark mood. She asked Niamh what was the matter and was even more insulted when Niamh just said, "I have got some thinking to do". "What" said D.F and just left Niamh on her own in the tent to her silly behaviour, she crawled into the next tent and Niamh could only hope that she enjoyed the experience despite the disaster. Niamh always felt guilty for the way she acted but if only she could tell her friend that she couldn't help it! She really tried to stop the demons from ruining her fun and keep her loved ones safe and it would be a couple of hours until Niamh finally dropped off exhausted again.

**Niamh felt that she had lost her friendship with DF after her strange behaviour in the tent that night.**

# Chapter 18

# SINISTER

As the weeks moved on so did Niamh's thoughts, to a different level. She developed comfort in fantasising about burning down the 'vile place' with everyone inside who had physically and mentally harmed her in her first two years at the school. Teachers and pupils alike would get the imaginary treatment. She agonised over how she would prevent a certain handful of people that she liked from attending school that day i.e. her cousin Joe, the beautifully spoken English teacher Mrs. Bleefully. "No, no" she thought to herself "that won't do, far too tricky and impossible ". So, she used the fantasy as a comfort and coping tool, the brilliant plan that never would come into fruition was of an ordinary day, maybe Monday morning, in the assembly hall at around 9.45 am. The unsuspecting thick *b*\*\*\*\*\*\*\* are singing their hypocritical hymns about faith, love and unity ... What a joke!

Niamh silently creeps up to the school hall doors and places a crow bar across the handles making it impossible to open from the inside. Then the best part, Niamh pours petrol under the doors and it swims like a river surrounding the scum inside, every *b*\*\*\*\*, every *b*\*\*\*\*\*\* who had invaded her space and attacked her, attacked her while she was minding her own business as she always was, attacked her when she got a sum wrong, attacked her when she spoke on rare occasions, who made fun of her or who simply ignored her. For the cocky brats who thought they were `God`s gift' to the opposite sex, for the teacher`s favourites, all of you can BURN IN HELL!! This fantasy was her best yet, everybody whom she despised in the `vile place 'paying the price for abusing Niamh.

If there was a pupil in the school whose mother had sadly died, this would send Niamh into total panic because of the fear of the same tragedy happening to her family. If the person in question moved in Niamh`s direction then she would quickly move out of the way as fast as she could, but she always did it discreetly as to not offend the bereaved person. Even though Niamh suffered sadistic thoughts she was a decent girl and she would never offend anybody she always clung to what her mother had told her "always treat people as you would want to be treated" and this is what Niamh and her sister did all their lives, so you can imagine how confused Niamh was when people didn't treat her as she would treat others. So, if some ones mother had died then Niamh had to make sure that she didn't `catch it'. The trick was that when she set eyes upon the poor person, she would instantly repeat the name of her enemies and think of their image in her head, this would put the curse of death upon them and not herself.

It is as though Niamh had the power to put bad luck onto her enemy`s and steer it away from herself. Niamh started to believe that she had special powers but only if she stuck to her rituals.

One very hot day when Niamh was sat down on the school lawn with a group of girls that she neither liked nor disliked, she had her long socks on and always made sure the hair on her legs didn't show, she would have loved to be able to wear short socks in the hot weather as every other girl that she saw around her was doing, but she was so embarrassed at the dark hairs on her legs, this was also why she wore long jogging bottoms for P.E. Suddenly a gentle breeze blew her skirt up and her legs were revealed. She quickly tried to pop her skirt back in place but one of the girls caught a glimpse of Niamh`s legs and started to laugh, "haven't you got hairy legs" said Marcia Canny, Niamh was furious, how dare this fat, spoilt brat say that and bring unwanted attention to Niamh`s unsightly legs and humiliate her in front of others.

**This was another incident of abuse towards Niamh and yet again there was NO ONE THERE to protect her!**

The next day Niamh was very cool with Marcia Canny and she made an unwitting remark about her to another pupil, it was something very trivial that Niamh couldn't even remember saying it, it was probably something to do with the incident the day before when Marcia laughed at Niamh`s hairy legs. Later that day while standing in line waiting to go into the classroom, Niamh felt a thud to her side, as she turned to see what had happened she saw Marcia standing there in a strop. "Don't you dare say that about me" she shouted as she punched Niamh`s school bag once again. The bag contained a compass and ruler and one of those items had struck Niamh`s rib cage through the fabric of the bag. "Ouch "she said to herself without showing any emotion, she didn't want this bitch to think she had succeeded in harming her. Marcia stood there proud as punch for putting Niamh in her place, Niamh just stared at her but in her mind she said to herself "you will die tonight". She couldn't wait to be alone in her bed, so she could chant her revenge and put a curse on Marcia.

***Even though Niamh's chanting and curses never made a difference, the people she hated always turned up for school very much alive, but it still gave great satisfaction to Niamh just to think about it!***

That night in bed Niamh made sure to take revenge on Marcia, she would chant her name and think of the people who had lost their mothers and hopefully the curse would fall on Marcia, this may seem very cruel and calculated but this is how the vile place had made Niamh and she had had enough of people abusing her, it was time to fight back. Marcia Canny was a spoilt brat, she had to have the best clothes, school bag, shoes and her hair was always done at the best hairdressers in the town. Marcia seemed to think that she had beautiful hair, but her hair was not what Niamh would ever wish for, it was uncontrollable, fizzy curls that you could never do anything with. Marcia seemed to think she was blessed, she was one of those girls who used Niamh if she didn't have any one to stand with in the playground or have dinner with, being billy- no- mate's just wasn't the done thing and girls would do anything to avoid this label. It was different for the boys, they could join in with the constant game of football life was so much easier for boys. It should be optional standing in the playground, Niamh always thought, there was nothing more depressing than standing huddled on a cold grey day in the playground. Why couldn't the pupils decide if they wanted to stay indoors or go outside? The six formers could stay in at break time, so why couldn't everyone else who wanted to stay in and keep warm?

Niamh despised and dreaded 'playtime', it wasn't playtime, it was horrible for her. At a glimpse of the clock she would have to start planning who she could stand next to even if she hated them. Niamh would look at the teachers in the staffroom through the window in the playground and she would despise them for being cosy and warm, sipping hot cups of tea. Niamh would fantasise that she was like the lead character in a movie she had seen the week before. Richard Burton was the star in *Midas Touch*, about a man who had special powers to destroy any building around him, Niamh wished the staff room roof to collapse and kill or injure all the cocky, arrogant sods underneath. With their degrees and big salaries, Niamh hated every one of them bar a couple, so she always made sure that her nice teachers were not in the staff room when she concentrated on bringing down the roof.

**Niamh always hung onto her mother's every word, and one of her sayings was "The Teachers bread is buttered, they don't care if you succeed or not, so work hard and one day your bread will be buttered, and you won't ever have to worry about money"**

## Chapter 19

# THE HOSPITAL

As soon as Niamh's parents realised something wasn't quite right with her behaviour they immediately got her to the Doctor. It was a relief and embarrassment at the same time for Niamh because she was certain the Doctor would laugh at her, but her parents assured her that he would get to the cause of this and make her better. "You must tell him everything about how you are feeling and the awful thoughts you are constantly having" said Kaitlyn to her daughter. "Me and dad are here with you and we want to help you all we can, so don't be embarrassed, everything will change from now on darling". The Doctor was very concerned, he wanted to get Niamh the best help as soon as possible, so he referred her to a Child psychologist at a Children's Hospital in the city. As her parents thanked the Doctor for his help and support they both sighed with relief, at last someone was going to make sense of all this and most important STOP their daughters suffering. The appointment card arrived in the post a week later, thanks to the G.P who requested an urgent response from the consultant in charge of the department at the hospital. Niamh was thrilled to have the day off school as they all set off for her very first visit to the child psychologist. It seemed a long way in the car, but Niamh didn't care, she was excited that she was going to be made normal and even more ecstatic that the delusions and demons would vanish from her mind forever.

They finally arrived at the car park, the place was huge, and it took them a while to find the waiting room they were meant to reporting to. "Niamh Conlen" a nice lady Doctor calls out the family followed her into a room that was pleasantly decorated with toys and pictures and bright coloured walls, Niamh felt instantly at ease and relaxed into the comfy chair she was sat on. This beautifully spoken lady was one of a team of consultants who specialise in mental illnesses` in children. This was told to Niamh`s parents while she was distracted by the I.Q test she had been set by the Doctor, she enjoyed the challenge and the puzzles and the general knowledge question`s, this was a chance for her parents to tell the Doctor exactly what had been going on.

They were beside themselves with worry, but they always kept their despair hidden from Niamh, the last thing they wanted was to add to her anxiety, if she thought for one minute that she was causing her parents stress and upset through her behaviour that would have tipped her over the edge and push her into deeper depression. The team of Doctors explored every avenue, they talked to both Kaitlyn and Sean together then separately to make sure and rule out any disfunction in their married life or the family as a unit, they even wanted to talk to little sis Lizzy to compare both sibling`s personality and again to rule out anything unpleasant going on in the family home. After the Doctors were satisfied that Niamh`s disorder was nothing to do with her family life, they decided to try her on medication. As they explained to Kaitlyn and Sean this would start off at a very low dosage and not to be alarmed. Sean was against the idea, he hated the idea of his child on medication, not the usual medicine for a cough or anti biotics for tonsillitis, no these were mind altering drugs to treat depression and personality disorders. It worried him greatly and saddened him deeply. "We have to try Sean" said Kaitlyn trying to be positive. "If these tablets make her better and happy then we have to let her go on them". As her parents, they had to sign that they give their consent in allowing the Doctors to treat Niamh with the drugs they thought best in conjunction with their diagnosis and that was personality disorder and emotionally immature. Strange, thought Niamh years later when her mother discussed the Doctors findings with her, how could an 11 year- old girl with sadistic fantasies of torture and murder be emotionally immature! One conclusion that Niamh had years later was that she wasn't totally honest with the Doctors. She didn't want to be taken away from her family so she kept her most sinister thoughts to herself!

# Chapter 20

# BRIDGET

Summer 1976, the Conlen family were settling down to watch the Saturday Night Movie when the phone rang, it was long distance and as usual it was Ireland calling. Sean answered and expected to be on the phone sometime chatting to his mother, sister, brother or a dear friend. It was his brother Garleth calling with worrying news that their alcoholic sister Bridget was spiralling out of control and the strain was having a devastating effect on their ageing mother Kathleen. Kathleen was a private woman who spent her days going to mass and reading the bible, so the news that her daughter was found drunk by the roadside in the early hours of the morning by the GARDA did not go down well with her and she needed a break. Bridget was a former beauty contestant and became miss Ireland with her raven black hair, olive skin and sharp good looks. She had the world at her feet, but, that 'ole devil called love' was her downfall! She met and fell in love with a married man who abruptly dropped her from a great height, so drink became her life and she lost everything, career, looks, respect and dignity.

So, the family in Ireland wanted rid of this embarrassment and insisted that Bridget come to England for Sean to share some of the responsibility.

After consulting with Kaitlyn, Sean agreed to have his sister stay with them for a few months and hopefully try to get her some help. The morning Bridget arrived it was a baking hot day and the pavements were cracking in the heat. She was stunning in a white suit with white high heels, she was the height of fashion and her black hair always cut well. Bridget was a trained hairdresser and ran a successful salon in her home town until the booze ruined her reputation. She was making mistakes on everything from perming, colours, cut and blows. She was almost sued for wrongly putting a bleach on a customer`s hair which caused it to fall out from burns to the scalp.

Niamh was so excited to have her favourite aunt come to stay for a while, but she would soon realise that they were both battling demons, but of a different kind. "I`m so thirsty" said Bridget after she had hugged and kissed the family upon her arrival. "I think I will take a walk to the shops and get some lemonade, maybe the kids would come with me". So, off the kids and aunt would go to the shop for lemonade. As they neared the shop Niamh stated that she wanted coke instead of lemonade, but aunt Bridget kept walking past the shop and said "we can sit outside the pub in the sunshine". Ok, thought the two girls who had brought a couple of their friends along from their street, this would be fun. Outside the pub on deck chairs they all sat happy in the sun and refreshed with their ice- cold drinks. Bridget was happy also, she had disguised a Brandy in her lemonade and that was her cunning plan to obtain alcohol without her brother Sean realising what she was up to. It soon became clear to Niamh that her aunt was suffering as well as herself.

When the group returned home after their trip to the local pub, it was obvious to Sean and Kaitlyn that Bridget was drunk. This was confirmed when Niamh told her parents where they had been on their little trip to the shop. Even though Bridget could disguise her drunk episodes well, her eyes were the give way, they would blink in slow motion when under the influence. This is how Sean always knew that she had been secretly drinking during the day.

It was decided that Bridget would sleep in the big bedroom with Niamh and Lizzy, there was room for three beds easily. The girls helped her to unpack and showed her which was her bed. Niamh noticed that Bridget quickly placed something under her pillow, when she asked what it was, Bridget just said it was her medicine that she had to take every night, it was a bottle of rum, just small enough to fit into a lady's handbag. After a long journey, Bridget was tired so she went to bed early, the girls were not far behind and soon the whole family were in bed. Niamh was woken in the night from sobbing coming from Bridget, she didn't say anything because she was embarrassed, so she pretended to be asleep. The smell of alcohol and the sound of lips meeting glass was prominent, suddenly Bridget spoke but not to Niamh, she was calling to her deceased father in heaven. "Daddy, daddy" is all she kept saying to herself. Niamh felt scared for a few minutes but then her fear turned to pity and sadness for a woman who was a frightened little girl wanting her dad to make everything better, like he did when she was a child.

The next day Niamh told her mother about what she heard, but Kaitlyn wasn't surprised because she had heard the stories about Bridget from the family in Ireland. So, a plan was needed to get Bridget back on the straight and narrow and off the drink.

Kaitlyn had arranged an interview for her at a trendy salon in the town who were looking for an experienced stylist, so off she went. When she returned later in the afternoon she proudly told the family that she had got a job! Everyone was over the moon, this could be a new beginning for Bridget. The weeks past and everything seemed fine and going well with the new job until Bridget started coming home later and later, she had begun to go for a `quick drink` after work into the pubs near the salon. Each day would be a different pub so not to draw attention to the woman sat on her own drinking Brandy every night after work. She would juggle the pubs to her advantage. This way the landlord would think that she came in to his bar once a week and same with the next landlord and the next. One -night Bridget was later than ever, and her brother Sean was very worried. He was pacing up and down and looking out of the window for her to walk around the corner. She finally turned up at 10. pm she opened the door in a very cheery, tipsy mood trying hard to conceal her guilty pleasure. "Where have you been?" asked Sean "I have been worried sick". Bridget laughed and shrugged it off. "I have been for a drink with the girls from work, and I have had my dinner so I will say good night and go to bed". Sean was furious, but what could he say, she was a grown woman, but she was also drunk, and you cannot reason with a drunk person. So, he thought it best to wait until the morning to confront her about her behaviour. The next day he approached Bridget before she set off to work and told her NOT to come home drunk after work. Bridget was offended but shrugged it off, as though she didn't want to draw attention to her disfunction. As sure as daylight she returned home late that night drunk. Sean couldn't hold back his disgust and he verbally blasted Bridget, he was angry and heart- broken at the same time. Bridget was his younger sister and he loved her dearly and felt a huge responsibility towards her. The family in Ireland could no longer cope with her but he was determined to sort her out some -how!

After a massive row with Sean, Bridget retreated to the bedroom where Niamh and Lizzy were sleeping. Niamh had earlier been battling her own demons in the mirror downstairs and it had taken her ages to get into bed. She was awakened by Bridget crying but sipping from a bottle of Rum at the same time. "Are you ok?" asked Niamh, "why are you crying?" Bridget stirred from her bed and moved over to Niamh for comfort. "I'm crying because I have made your father hate me" she said. "No, don't be silly Daddy doesn't hate you, he's just worried about you and he is worried about me also"! Bridget hugged Niamh close and said "Darling angel, I know you are suffering these silly thoughts, your exhausted, my poor girl, but listen to me and remember my words when the time comes. One day you will be beautiful, you are going to be so beautiful and everyone will want to be your friend, everyone will love you and all this will be forgotten". Both Niamh and Bridget began to cry, for themselves and for each other. They were aunt and niece struggling addiction and disorder.

*When the time came that Niamh blossomed into a beautiful young woman, she couldn't understand why boys were suddenly interested in her and every boy wanted to take her out on a date. It took some time before it dawned on her what her Aunt's words were ... "One day you will be beautiful" ...*

# Chapter 21

# **THE CHOIR**

End of summer and Niamh was depressed at the thought of going back to the vile place, it was a new school term and she would be a second- year pupil. This was the time of year when the music teachers were looking for candidates to join the choir in preparation for the Christmas carol service. An older girl called Jeanie Greeves had befriended Niamh on the bus at home time, she was a decent girl and she was also from the same village as Niamh, so they had got chatting on the journey to and from school. Jeanie was a bubbly girl but absolutely 'boy crazy', she made Niamh laugh on many occasion with her flirting and plans to get certain boys to fancy her. Niamh enjoyed her company so much on the bus that she wished the bus ride wouldn't end and they didn't have to go their separate ways in the school. Jeanie was a year older and had her own best friend Angela Hawsby, who was a bit jealous of Niamh and tended to be bitchy with her on a few occasions. This didn't really worry Niamh because she knew that Jeanie wouldn't let Angela go too far in her resentment of her. So, Jeanie and Angela decided to join the choir again for a second time, they had signed up last year simply to get out of lessons because there was so much rehearsing to be done before Christmas. "Why don't you join with us?" asked Jeanie to Niamh. Niamh hated the sound of her own voice and simply said "I can't sing". "Neither can we, we just mime, it's great, you can miss loads of *s\*\*\** lessons" replied Jeanie. This immediately appealed to Niamh so she gladly became a member of St. Gonner's Choir.

The new choir assembled in the hall for practise, seeing as they were to perform in the local church for the public, the head master didn't object to pupils missing lessons because they were to be the ambassadors of the school and make him proud and look good in the local newspaper. Niamh thought this was great, no maths, no P.E, no horrible pupils that she hated she was over the moon and Jeanie was there to make her laugh which made it even better. It amused Niamh that the music teachers had no idea that half of their group couldn't sing or even wanted to sing. There were no boys in the choir just girls, some older than Niamh and some were new to the school, first years.

One morning while the choir was singing hymns in front of the whole school, this was also why a choir was needed to lead in morning prayers because the rest of the school just couldn't be bothered, and this led to a fiery outburst by one of the music teachers Mr. Kallum, he would lose his rag many a time over poor performances and insist on a re-play, in front of the head teacher as well, who himself was taken back by this hysterical re action. Just before the headmaster entered the hall, the whole school were chatting among themselves and the choir was warming up. Niamh was sat next to Jeanie as usual and Angela was sat at the other side of Jeanie as usual. Suddenly a voice from behind spoke to Jeanie, "Eh this *is f\*\*\*\*\*\** great, no *f\*\*\*\*\*\** lessons, we've just joined to *p\*\*\** about and get out of lessons". Jeanie replied in a much refiner voice to the low life scum sat behind her "Yes me and Angie and Niamh have done the same thing". "Who`s this? "asked the scum bag "This is Niamh, she`s a second year, she`s my friend and she`s joined with me. The next instant Niamh felt a heavy thud to the back of her head, she was spun into dizziness and the pain made her feel sick, she was seeing double as she slowly turned around to see who had assaulted her AGAIN! What she saw was two fat, ugly thick as poo, pieces of *** girls who were older than herself and laughing at what one of them had just done to the girl with her back to them which was Niamh. Jeanie went quiet with shock, she couldn't believe what these monster`s had done to her friend, even Angie put her head down in sympathy. Niamh felt that Jeanie was intimidated by these low life`s and was afraid to react, she knew them just because they were in her form class but the association ended there.

That night at home, Niamh`s rituals were running havoc with her mind, she couldn't wait to get into the shower and wash her hair, wash the contamination off from the scum who had attacked her that morning. She felt dirty and infected and each time she scrubbed and rinsed then scrubbed and rinsed she cursed the girls over and over, she thought if she cursed hard enough the two wouldn't see another day or better still be crushed under a bus so they could never walk again. Niamh would take great satisfaction from seeing them struggling around the school in wheel chairs. Wishful thinking as always!

The next day Niamh told Jeanie that she didn't want to continue in the choir due to what had happened to her the day before, but Jeannie wanted her to stay a member, she tried to assure Niamh that it will be ok, but Niamh wasn't happy at all. A few days went by and Jeanie had some good news for Niamh, the low life scum who attacked her were kicked off the choir for messing about and not taking it seriously. So, Niamh was over the moon and reinstated herself in the choir.

**Niamh began to think that she was the one who was cursed, she just could not understand why people kept attacking her at random!**

# Chapter 22

# THE STAIRS

Niamh was struggling getting up the stairs at bed time, this may seem ludicrous, but it was a nightmare for her, it was the most difficult part of her day. It was bad enough getting past the delusional demons in the mirror but now she had to keep going up and down the stairs until she acquired order in her mind. This was time consuming mental torture. She would gear herself up about half an hour before her parents said would be time for bed. Her father Sean wasn't happy with her behaviour but since Niamh had been under the care of the child psychiatrist at the hospital he had become more understanding, but Niamh still did her best to hide her rituals from her parents. It would start with a glass of milk, piece of toast for supper, as soon as her father brought the plate of toast and drinking chocolate or hot milk into the lounge for herself and her sister, Niamh knew she had to prepare for battle. She would feel the anxiety starting to swell in her head and the butterflies in her tummy. Would she make it to bed in 10 minutes, 15 minutes, 20 minutes or an HOUR? "Ok up to bed both of you" the words from her parents that she dreaded every night. "Night, night, strait into bed now Niamh, remember what the Doctor said, don't give in to the rituals, if you ignore them then they will disappear." Niamh hadn't been prescribed any medication at this stage, she was having weeks of therapy, tests and counselling until the Doctors knew what medication would be the right course of treatment to make her better. After her sister had climbed the stairs and got into bed Niamh followed, she would pretend to be fine and get into bed, but she knew she couldn't fall asleep without carrying out her rituals and make sure her family was safe. 2pm and all the family were fast asleep, all except poor little Niamh, she would wait until she could hear snoring coming from all bedrooms and then she slowly and quietly crept out of bed. Every step was like walking in a mine field, she couldn't let her parents down, they had been so worried, and they believed that the worst was over, but it wasn't it was worse than ever. "Nearly reached the stairs now" she said to herself, careful not to the step on the creaky floor board that she knew so well, careful not to wake grandad up or cause the dogs to bark. Each step took ages, her heart was racing, she was cold, she was too anxious to even pop her nice warm dressing gown on, she just wanted to get the deed done. At last she was at the top of the stair case, slowly carefully down each step. She would start to sweat with the intensity as though she was diffusing a bomb. A slight noise stopped her in her tracks "please don't wake up, please, please don't wake up" she whispered to herself. 15 minutes passed as she stood in silence on the stairs, cold and tired but determined. Half an hour passes and she is only half way down the stairs, she sits down in exhaustion. 15 minutes pass and she continues step by step until finally she reaches the bottom. Once there she had to stand in front of the mirror in the hall, staring and organising at she looks at her reflection, first she has to convince herself that she is in control and that could take 30 minutes or more, second she has to diminish the images of all the pupils and teachers at St, Gonner's whom she despised with festering loathing. Opening and closing her eyes countless times trying to get the correct image in the mirror and in her mind, these were the passport's for sleep and until she had endorsed them she wasn't going anywhere but staying put at the foot of the stairs and in front of the mirror. 2 hours would pass, and Niamh was asleep on the landing as she was many times before, she would persist until she could no longer keep her eyes open. She would wake up usually with the dawn because she subconsciously knew that she had to get back into bed before her parents woke so they would think that she had had a good night's sleep and a sure sign that she was getting better, but she would get much worse before she would get better.

**What could she do to make herself normal, no matter how hard she tried, things just went from bad to worse.**

# Chapter 23

# DOWN AGAIN

Niamh welcomed every opportunity to get out of lesson's, so she was relieved that she was back in the choir and more so that the two girls who had viciously thumped her in the head were out! It was September 1976 and the new term meant that she was moved up into the big school yard which she hated. She would often look across at the new intake of pupils in the first- year yard and wondered how they were settling in to new school trauma. She had no empathy with them just morbid curiosity! Where any of them being bullied? Did they cry themselves to sleep at night? Probably not!

So, the one consolation of the big school yard was that Niamh could be with Jeanie whom she enjoyed being with and felt secure with. Every day at break time she would make her way to the yard and find Jeanie. Cold, miserable winter days were spent huddled up together in the entrance door way. Even though Niamh felt depressed not only because she hated school but she was also suffering from visual depression, this was caused by the lack of sunshine and grey, dull, rainy weather which in later years would be labelled as 'Seasonal Affected Disorder' or SAD. The only relief she had was the laughter caused by Jeanie's funny stories of the boys she had dated and wanted to date. Jeanie would also make up funny names for the many horrible teachers in the school and tell how she would pull her tongue out at them when they weren't looking. As the new term went on it would soon be time to start revision for the upcoming exams to determine who was working hard and who wasn't. Again, the last in the pecking order would go down to the lower sets and the top swat would move up to the higher sets. Niamh pushed this thought to the back of her mind, she had the notion that she wouldn't be going down again surely, but then on the other hand she didn't really care, the only thing that worried her was the embarrassment if she was put down again! She had developed a way of conning the teachers into thinking that she was concentrating on lesson and doing her work, this involved writing a word or two in her note pad and then just keep writing the same word over and over or writing over the same word. This started off as a ritual while battling disturbing thoughts in her head but then she soon discovered that it kept the teachers at bay. It must have looked to them that Niamh was in deep concentration and a keen learner. Strange, that none of them picked up on the inner turbulence that Niamh was experiencing by the state of her work! Surely, they would have questioned why she was scribbling the same word again and again or making the word unreadable because it had been written over and over and was a thick mass of ink! No, it seemed that Niamh had slipped under the radar or wasn't that important enough to retrieve. Not a top learner or achiever, not expected to `do well'. Maybe if she had been a pretty boy footballer or a top gymnast or the leading girl in the latest school production of `Joseph and his technicoloured dream coat', no, she wasn't any of these. She also never flirted with the school's lady's man or sucked up to the `perfect prefect' no she certainly didn't do any of these. All she thought about all day long was home time.

The Autumn days were getting shorter and the run up to Christmas had begun. Niamh loved the four months before Christmas, she loved the fantasy and the decorations, tinsel and glitter, even the school assembly hall seemed a nicer place to be with a huge Christmas tree dominating the stage. The Choir had started to visit the local church to practise with the organ and test out the acoustic's for the carol service to be held there. This also meant that they could go home early rather than trail all the way back to school for the last hour before home time. Rumour was that the two music teachers in charge of the choir were having an affair both were unhappily married to their oblivious spouses and judging by the amount of time they spent together in school, always together in the staff room, nipping out together at lunch time, well, it was obvious. These two individuals were Mrs. Higham and Mr. Boon, they were very suited to each other, both arrogant, self -indulgent, in- sensitive, up their own bums, pair of snobs you could ever meet. Even though it was thanks to them that Niamh could skip lessons due to practising for the Carol service, she didn't like them, they were never nasty to Niamh, but they were never nice to her either. In fact, she found them laughable when Jeanie would make fun of them because they had no idea that everybody suspected them of having an adulteress relationship.

Exam week comes around fast and furious, the teachers were putting the final revisions into place, after all if they have too many failures then they will have the head master to answer to and they certainly didn't want that. They covered everything from division to literature capital cities to past prime ministers, but not for Niamh, every word they said just went right over her head, didn't register, the lights were on but nobody's home, in one ear, out the other! Monday morning, first exam, Monday afternoon, second exam and so on and so on until last exam Friday afternoon. Home time and Niamh is hurrying to the town centre bus station to catch up with Jeanie for the journey home. On the bus, Jeanie and a few other friends are discussing the weeks gruelling tests and wondering and hoping if they have done well or not. Niamh doesn't comment she just listens, it doesn't have any impact on her or concern, she just wants to get home and put her uniform into the washing machine for her mother to wash and then she can get into her bathroom to shower and scrub herself with disinfectant then pop on her pyjamas and settle down on the settee with her family and dogs and cats.

Two weeks passed since the exams and Niamh was anxiously awaiting the teachers to read out each pupil's results to the whole class, not because she was worried about coming last in everything because she expected that, but she was dreading the humiliation of being the class dunce and everyone laughing at her. She knew that the teachers didn't care who was ridiculed for coming last, in fact she suspected that they looked on it as a punishment for not working hard and revising. As sure as anything Niamh was right to worry, she came last in everything and once again the teachers read out the names from highest scorer to dunce which again was poor Niamh. So, as expected this meant that she was going down again, this time to C group. She knew of the pupils in C group and quite liked them when she had mingled with them in various lessons i.e P.E and religion, she didn't dislike them and they seemed to treat her with respect, which was a rare thing for Niamh. No one in the top class had ever treated her with respect in the 12 months that she had been at the vile place. Niamh put this down to the fact that the lower classes were humble and homely, but the higher classes were arrogant and detestable. Niamh knew which group she preferred to be in and it wasn't the scum in the top set. After the initial humiliation was over and everyone had a good laugh at Niamh's 'fall from grace' again, she was quite excited about moving down to C, simply because she thought she might be happier with a nice bunch of kids and she could finally get away from those she hated for good.

***Apart from the humiliation of coming last again, Niamh couldn't be happier moving down to C group, this is not the mind of a normal child, who would be glad to be going down again?!***

# Chapter 24

# STORM AND KERRY

September 1977, Niamh and her family were religiously attending counselling and cognitive behaviour therapy to hopefully put an end to Niamh's disturbing, tormenting thoughts and pointless rituals. At the same time at home there was some exciting news, the 2 family pets German Shepherd dog's Storm and Kerry were to become proud parents of a litter of pups. The family were so excited at the thought of pitter, patter from tiny, fairy paws, even Sean had got used to the idea after being annoyed when the pair accidentally got together after three weeks of successfully keeping them apart, only to be mated because somebody left the garden gate open leading to the dog's outdoor play area and as quick as a flash they were stuck together reproducing!

At the hospital, the child psychologist finally decided on the best course of medication to halt Niamh's depression and disorder, ` Seratin 'would be the powerful weapon to get the job done and achieve the result they were after. So, it was decided that Niamh would start the course immediately. The Doctors were satisfied that Niamh's irrational behaviour and black moods had nothing to do with any family abuse or neglect, they stated that this was caused by a chemical imbalance that she was born with and this also contributed to her mood swings depending on the weather. The lack of Seratin in Niamh's brain was causing her to wish she was dead with each dull, rainy day. These new drugs would also combat her compulsions to repeat actions and hopefully the misery would end.

One weekend Niamh`s mother Kaitlyn suggested that they all took up swimming at the local pool, she thought this would be good for Niamh. Friday night would be the night for the swimming session, so off they went mother and daughters and a couple of friends who requested to come along. As Niamh was undressing she suddenly became aware of the amount of hairs on her legs, they seemed to have multiplied over- night, her heart sank. "No" she frantically repeated to herself, "what`s wrong Niamh?" said her mother "Everything is wrong with me" she said to herself, but to her mother she just said "nothing". Whilst in the swimming Pool, Niamh thought she would see other teenage girls with hairs on her legs, so she discreetly surveyed them. She looked at arms and legs and to her horror she found no hairs on any girl she looked at, not one. I am a freak she thought, I am a FREAK!

The only reasonable explanation for this was that Niamh had very dark skin from her Mediterranean ancestry and body hair went with the genetics whether you were male or female. While swimming around in the water, Niamh commented on the strong smell of bleach in the air, her mother explained to her that the smell was bleach also named as chlorine. Niamh liked the smell, and even more when her mother told her that it purified everything that it touched, killed germs and cleaned intensively. This led to a rota of Niamh attending the swimming pool every week, even if the others didn't go, it became an obsession for Niamh to thoroughly cleanse herself every Friday afternoon of the stench, grit and grime of the vile place. She adored the smell of chlorine and bleached appearance of her skin after an hour in the water, so this ritual was a must for the foreseeable future.

Niamh had noticed the adverts on TV about women shaving their legs, when she discussed this with her mother, she dismissed the idea as not good because it would make the hairs grow back stronger. "No, don't ever do that" said Kaitlyn "It'll make the problem worse". Niamh took this advice on board but she didn't abide with it. One miserable, rainy, day Niamh was in her bathroom, staring at her legs and hating them with her soul. In a bout of delusion and depression she took her father's shaving blade and foam and obliterated every hair on her legs as though she was cutting their throats. After the deed was done, she sat back and sighed with relief, the evil hairs had finally gone, but poor Niamh didn't realise that the hairs would grow back thicker than ever, her mother's words didn't quite make sense when she warned her about shaving. "Once done, twice the work" she would say.

Niamh's legs were a mass of blood spots all running in to each other, the sting was nasty and for a moment she started to panic, she had no choice but to tell her mother what she had done. "You stupid girl" said Kaitlyn "Why have you done that?" Niamh burst into tears, and wished she could turn the clock back. "I hate my legs and arms, they are not normal, why am I not blonde? why am I not white?" The delusion that she was black was dominant in her mind but this wasn't the case, the family were of Irish and Mediterranean ancestry and this was the reason for Niamh`s dark skin, hair and eyes. Because of her obsession with the Swedish super group Abba, Niamh wanted to be blonde with blue eyes and what she was, she wasn't happy with … at all! Every time she looked in the mirror she wanted to vomit because she hated the image that stared back at her. "You *f\*\*\*\*\*\** freak, you don't deserve to live, you are too *f\*\*\*\*\*\** ugly for this world, get lost, was all she could scream in desperation. "Why are you doing this to me? I am Swedish, I have blonde hair and blue eyes, you can`t do this to me"! "Get the *f\*\*\** away from me before I kill you," she ranted at her reflection. On many occasion Niamh wanted to kill herself, but as always she spared her parents the pain of finding their beloved daughter hanging from the loft hatch door. The loft hatch door was the ideal place to hang herself, Niamh decided, the strong wooden foundation would me more than enough strength to hold a 13 - year old girl.

So, Niamh had started her medication, by now Christmas was looming once again and before long the new litter of pups were due to be born. November, and the mother to the pups was acting weird, constantly licking her private parts, collecting clothing and placing it in a quiet corner of the house, under the stairs was the chosen spot. Sean knew instantly what was happening and immediately made a comfortable nest in the wooden shed outside in the garden. "There now girl, you will be undisturbed and peaceful here, I will keep looking in on you to see if your babies have arrived" Sean said calmly to Kerry, mother to be. Every hour he would check on Kerry, one after another they arrived, not one or two but eight beautiful healthy, chunky pups were born and the whole family were so delighted. Kerry was given extra food and milk to help her cope with the demand of feeding such a huge number of offspring. Storm the proud father was kept at bay for the time being because Kerry would not be happy with him poking his nose in while her pups were so young, he would soon get to meet his children when the time was right. "Can we see them? Can we see them daddy?" said Niamh and Lizzy. "Not yet" said Sean in a responsible voice, "Kerry will be upset if we all start touching her pups and she may eat them in fear". At this realization, all the family left well alone and retreated to the living room to discuss names for the new arrivals.

*Even though Niamh fantasised about killing herself on many occasion, the only thing that stopped her was the pain that would cause to her family, so this was her safety net.*

# Chapter 25

# SNOW AND ABBA

The week before Xmas and school holidays was nearly here. Niamh was so excited not only because it was Xmas but the fact she had two whole weeks off to look after the pups that had been born a couple of weeks before. Kerry the German Shepherd dog who was the proud Mother of the pups had accepted the whole family in caring for her pups. She welcomed the intervention of making sure that each pup got its fill of milk by Niamh or Lizzy swapping one` full up' pup on the teat to the smaller, weaker pup getting its fill. By now Kerry was getting tired of the demands made on her and so she welcomed the special formula milk that Sean would make up for the pups. More and more she left the feeding to Sean and Niamh and so the pups grew stronger and stronger with each day. By Xmas eve the pups were toddling around and their eyes were wide open, they recognised the family and as soon as they saw them they would run to them with tails wagging and looking to be fed. They were eight bundles of fluff and fun. To make Xmas even more magical it snowed and snowed and snowed. "Yes, yes" said Niamh," Father Xmas will be able to get here easily on his sledge". Niamh always held on to the fantasy that Santa Claus was real, to admit that he wasn't was too painful a thought to even dare to imagine. So, the fantasy went on and on for many years.

Niamh had requested to her parents that they send the new album from Abba to father Xmas. `Arrival' was the best-selling disc of the year. Abba was the biggest name on the planet and their army of fans had grown to universal size, so everybody wanted the magic and music heaven brought into their homes. This was a `must have' Xmas present of every- body's list. But for Niamh it was more of a present under her tree, it was a way of life, of living every song on the album and escaping into that magical, wonderful world of these super Swedes. She imagined their world would be of mountains, forests, lakes and trees with everybody in their world being blonde with blue eyes and reindeers and mystical eagles who could talk. It would be `**Narnia**` meets` **The singing ringing tree**` and **Pippy long-stocking**` all wrapped in one. For those of you who haven't heard of the above, they were kid's stories of the time, only Narnia was brought back into the lime light years later.

Xmas morning was always `heaven on earth ` for Niamh but this time was special because she had been granted her wish, the Abba disc was there under the tree just waiting to be played on the player standing by in the corner of the room. Niamh played it over and over and over again, her parents were quite sick of the thing after an hour or so, but Niamh was happy and that was all that mattered. Sean and Kaitlyn had no idea what importance Abba had to Niamh, they just thought she was another teenager with a crush on the latest pop band.

To add to the joy of Xmas the snow was tumbling down and before long it was two- foot deep, the garden and street were suddenly transformed into the mountains of Sweden and the country of `Narnia`. Niamh and Lizzy spent Xmas day playing out on the street with friends, pulling sledges up and down the path and making snow men. Niamh and Lizzy asked their Father could they bring the pups out to play with them and show them off to their friends. "Ok said Sean but keep good care of them." "We promise, we promise, thankyou dad" the girls shouted with joy. So, one by one the chunky pups were introduced to the world, they ran up and down with the kids, they were given rides on the sledges and they chased snowballs, they were having a great time and so was Niamh. At this point, Niamh did not realise that she was enjoying herself, it was only hearing her Parents discussing her progress with the Child psychologist the following week that she was told that she had improved in her mental health. That was why she was feeling good about life, she did wonder why? The medication was starting to work, and Niamh didn't notice the decline in her rituals and torment. Her Parents were over the moon, they couldn't believe the difference in her, she had shown an interest in normal activities other than her pattern of disorder.

**Unwitting to Niamh, she was getting better.**

# Chapter 26

# HEART ATTACK

Everything seemed to be going smooth for a while in Niamh's life, the medication had started to work, and she was over the moon with the new puppies. Bridget was still living with the family and sadly she hadn't improved with her drinking habit and her demons were still torturing her. One night when Niamh and Lizzy were at home with their father Sean and their Aunt Bridget, it was obvious that Bridget was drunk as usual but maybe a bit worse. Kaitlyn was working late at the factory making exhaust pipes for cars, Sean wasn't happy at this because it was the era of the serial killer 'Jack the Ripper', but the family were planning a holiday in Cornwall that coming summer and they needed every penny. The house door opened and there was Bridget, she stood staring at Sean and the two girls as they watched TV. "Hello" she said, slurring her voice, "I am trying to phone heaven to speak to my Daddy, but I can't get through". Sean looked at his Sister with great sadness, he could not believe things had got so bad. "Don't be silly Bridget "he said wearily," our Father is DEAD"!!! "Yes, I know that Sean, that is why I am trying to contact him". At this point Sean couldn't help but retaliate and he started a heated argument with his alcoholic Sister. The situation went from bad to worse and soon Bridget was on her hands and knees crying into the phone handset. "Daddy, daddy, where are you"? This was too much for Sean to bear and he broke down in tears, he started with chest pain and a tightening in his arm. "Go and get your Mother" he said to the girls, "tell her to come home quickly". Straight away the girls got their two protective German Shepherd dogs and ran up the street to where the factory was that their Mother was working in. "Mum, mum, you have to come home now, Daddy is ill and Bridget is drunk". Kaitlyn left the factory straight away and they all headed for home. On her arrival, she found a worrying site, Bridget was crying and still shouting abuse at Sean but he was slumped on the kitchen chair sweating and in pain. "Ambulance, ambulance, please come quickly, I think my husband is having a heart attack".

Two days passed, and Sean was still in hospital, he was 33 years old and had just suffered a 'warning' to his health, his body was telling him that his life was in danger if he didn't stop worrying and taking all this stress on board. There was nothing else for it, Bridget had to go! So, Kaitlyn phoned the family in Ireland to tell them that their Brother had nearly had a bad heart attack due to the stress of Bridget, worrying and arguing, so, she would be on the next boat home as soon as her bags were packed. And they were packed, as soon as Kaitlyn got home she arranged for a taxi to take Bridget to the train station then onto the Irish Ferries in Liverpool. Everything must be calm for Sean when he got home. Poor Sean, the strain on him had taken its toll, it was bad enough having an alcoholic Sister but worse for him was the fact that his thirteen- year- old Daughter Niamh was suffering from a Mental Illness and he felt helpless at times to help her.

*So, Bridget was gone bit the worry for Sean was still there*.

# Chapter 27

# C GROUP AND FRANCINE

New term, new year 1977. Niamh was optamistic about going down to the next form class C. She had an insight into the kind of people in there and she hoped she would be happy with them. She was right, the kids in the lower sett were so different, they were friendly and funny and welcoming to Niamh. She also had an incline that a few of the boys fancied her. This was through an` off the cuff `comment that one of the girls had told her. Some of the other girls were asking the boy most fanciable in C form who would he `go out with' if he could. "I`m not sure" was his reply, "maybe Niamh Conlen". Niamh was astounded that any boy would fancy her let alone the class `heart throb'!

After that Niamh began to notice the boy more, just to observe his reaction toward her. It was always with a blush that he spoke to her and he was always trying to make her laugh. In the end Niamh shrugged it off as her imagination but she was still bewildered that anybody would fancy her with her black curly hair, dark eyes and skin, she was far from the `blonde bombshells' that graced the school by their presence. In C class Niamh became friendly with another quiet girl with a similar personality to her- self. Francine Sillan was a half Irish, half Italian girl. She was very quiet, maybe quieter than Niamh and she had no confidence what so ever, so she warmed to Niamh straight away. In -fact

Niamh was the only person that Francine would ever talk to but she never got bullied for being introvert like Niamh did, no, the kids in C form just respected that Francine was quiet and they left her in peace. Both girls had black, curly hair, dark eyes and skin but Francine didn't suffer the body hair on her arms and legs as Niamh did, Niamh could never understand this, why was Niamh afflicted with this horrible defect? That is how Niamh saw it as an **AFFLICTION!**

Niamh and Francine got on so well because maybe they had one huge thing in common, **hatred**, for the school they shared. Ironically Francine was also unhappy when she was away from her family, she loved her Parents and Siblings as Niamh did and she spent her school day being miserable. Of all her lessons Francine hated P.E the most, not the activities but the teacher, the evil Miss.C and her evil cronies. Francine told Niamh that a few months before they had become friends she had told Miss. C that she wasn't joining in the P.E lesson on that certain day because she was on her period and her Mother said that she would write a note and explain to the teacher that Francine feels very uncomfortable while jumping on the trampoline while on her periods, which speaks for itself! Miss C. wasn't having any of this and threatened that if Francine didn't undress and change from uniform to P.E kit, then she would physically` do it for her'. Poor Francine had no choice, she was terrified of the` **Witch'** and reluctantly got undressed. When hearing of this, Francine's Mother was fuming and came to the school to complain. As usual, the Head Master smoothed it over and that was the end of it, but Francine never forgot, and she despised **ALL** the P.E Instructors from that day on.

One afternoon in the Gym hall playing Netball, the C Group girls were having fun trying to get the ball in the high net and for once Francine was coming out of herself because of Niamh. She felt like she had a `**comrade in arms'**, herself and Niamh against the teachers. Even the other girls in the group commented on how Francine was a different person since Niamh came into their form class, they said they had never heard her speak before or laugh. Niamh felt good about this, she felt useful. So, Wednesday afternoon and Miss. Latex is laying down the rules of Netball. She wasn't a nice woman, she never smiled or had any fun with the girls, she was a miserable, bad tempered sod. "Listen when I am talking," is all she could shout!! "Right, when I blow my whistle, I want silence". Just as she blew her whistle Niamh and Francine laughed at each other trying to stand on one leg, it was nothing to do with Miss. L, they weren't laughing at her or being disrespectful it was a pure `**fluke'**, it was literally a few seconds over the last sound of the whistle. "Right, you two come here, now". The whole class fell deadly silent as Miss. L`s voice rang in echo through the acoustics of the building. "Bend over both of you" she said spitefully. Niamh was the first to step forward when Francine shouted "No! we haven`t done anything ". "Don't you dare give me cheek, that's two belts for even thinking about answering me back" said Miss. L, in a vengeful voice. So, Niamh would once again be assaulted for a very minor era. After the `attack' Francine said to Niamh quickly, "don't show her that she has hurt you, rub your bum and it will stop hurting". So, the two girls in pain put on a brave face and they didn't give Miss. L, the satisfaction of seeing them squirm.

The next day Francine decided that she was NEVER going to P.E lesson again and she came up with a plan. If herself and Niamh offered to take messages from one teacher to another then they could walk the corridors during P.E time and have the excuse that they were on an 'errand 'for which ever teacher wanted to send a note to the office or somewhere else in the school building. Niamh liked this idea very much even though she was nervous when they were doing it. "Don't worry Niamh, it will be fine, I promise" said Francine. Well, that was enough encouragement for Niamh and she happily went along with it. The pair of them would offer to run errands for the teachers and after a while the sight of them both walking around the school with a note in their hand was their passport for 'freedom'. The rooms they would walk past in view of the resident teacher inside just became the norm. Once or twice they were asked what they were doing but Francine just swiftly flashed a blank piece of paper and that was enough to passify the enquirer. A lot of the time the 'erronds' were legitimate but soon they became confident enough to walk around with the 'blank paper' trick and so they managed to 'dodge' P.E again and again. They both knew that there were only a few months left of having to do P. E because when they reached '3rd Year' they would not be choosing the activity for their G.C.S.E exams so they didn't need to learn what the 'evil witches' had to show them and who could blame them. Assaulted, humiliated, perved at in the shower, no, not for them two. Soon they would become more daring and venture up into the town and walk around the shops, get chips for dinner and coke to drink. Niamh loved this, she felt that she was in control of her life, she didn't want to be in the 'vile place' and Francine had given her confidence and know how to do it. Francine may have been a bad influence on Niamh but Niamh was over the moon to have her as a friend. The thing was that if Niamh had been happy at that school then she would have worked hard but all she knew was bullying by pupils and teachers and the fact that she had been **physically assaulted 8 times!!**

So, as time went on it came to the attention of the school that Niamh and Francine were truanting, and the game was up. Niamh`s parents were very disappointed and concerned at the same time. In a bout of tears Niamh explained to them how she had been un happy all through- out her 2 years at the school and that she hated everybody in the place. "I will take you away and you can go to a different school" said Kaitlyn. The school of choice was in another town and about the same distance from the town the `**vile place'** was. Some of the kids from her street were at this new school and Niamh and her parents thought she would be happy there. She could travel there with her friends and hopefully settle down and work hard. Kaitlyn and Sean took Niamh to view the new school, they met the head teacher and they were shown around the place. Niamh liked the situation of the school because it was more in the countryside and not next to a smelly abottoir or paper mill. The next day Kaitlyn rang the school and told them she was taking Niamh away, even though Niamh had told her parents she was un happy there, she didn't tell them about the abuse she had endured from teachers and pupils, again she didn't want them to worry, especially after her Father had not long suffered a heart-attack through worrying about her.

The headmaster from the 'vile place' requested a meeting with Niamh and her Parents to discuss was there anything he could do to change their minds. "We don't want to lose good girls like Niamh" was his opening words, this annoyed Niamh because it simply wasn't true. She thought the Head master couldn't care less about Niamh, in fact she thought that he didn't even know that she existed. Why did he never stop her in the corridors and ask her was everything ok, no, never. He just didn't want this to look bad on the school. He had his head in the clouds most of the time and didn't know half that went on during the day. Why didn't he intervene when she was attacked by evil Mrs. P, and that b****** Mr. F? So, that evening the family sat down at the dinner table and discussed Niamh's options. Would she be 'out of the fat and into the fire'? The words from the head teacher rang out in Niamh's mind and her Parents. "What should she do"? Finally, they all decided that it could be far worse for her to leave the 'vile place'. "Better the devil you know" said her Mother Kaitlyn "I'm worried about your future, I don't want you being disrupted and this affect your G.S.C.E s". So, after all that Niamh stayed at the vile place.

One of the problems for Niamh was the dinner hall, she hated having to go there for meals, it was a war zone just to get in the door. So, her Mother came up with the idea of packed lunch and Niamh was relieved. The next day she happily sat in the cloak room having her sandwiches with like- minded people who also hated the dinner que. There she became friendly with a couple of 'nice' girls and for a while she was settled. She still always felt that she was used from time to time by girls who's 'bezzy' mate was off school, and they just wanted someone to stand next to in the play-ground or sit and have lunch with. Niamh missed Francine because after the truanting phase the teachers did their best to keep them apart. So, they drifted, and Francine found a new friend.

*Niamh had never been happier than her time with Francine, but the teachers were watching them, just to spoil their FUN.*

# Chapter 28

# PERIODS

Niamh was 13 now and had not yet started her periods, she had found it traumatic to have to wear a bra when her Mother decided it was time. She questioned to herself why do women have to wear bras and have periods? She resented boys who seemed to sail through puberty without hassle. It was bad enough developing body hair and not just on her legs. She hated her growth of pubic hair, she found it repulsive. At school, she would hear stories of girls who had started their period for the first time while sitting at their desks. This played on Niamh`s mind constantly. The fear of losing blood and not knowing that it was seeping all over the classroom floor. These were the scary stories that had been circulating among pre-menstrual girls and the older girls made it worse by telling the younger girls that it was `horrible' and `embarrassing'! Another girl said that she was on the trampoline during P.E and her period started through the physical exertion. Niamh developed an obsession that she had blood in her pants and a tweaking vaginal pain, though she didn't know what a vagina was at the time. Every single time that she stood up from her desk chair she would cautiously check the seat to make sure there was no blood there. This went on for months, she also hated the embarrassment of having to tell her Mother when the time came. It was a nightmare for her, on top of everything else. All through the summer months she was afraid to wear shorts or thin trousers in case it started, and she would be humiliated. She didn't realise that it doesn't work like that, as every woman knows, it starts with a little blood and builds up to a heavy flow.

One day as she was walking from classroom to classroom she felt a slight pain in her groin area, she was sure that this was it and in despair she examined herself discreetly, but some cocky boy spotted her and said, "stop playing with your crutch". Niamh looked at him with HATRED, if she could have sent down a bolt of lightning to strike him DEAD then she would have gladly. She disliked this boy immensely because he thought he was God's gift **(not for Niamh, but for most of the girls in the year)** he was big headed and loved himself and he was a cocky sod. Also, this individual took Niamh's place in A group, as Niamh spiralled down in her grades this b****** ascended in his grades, he seemed to have everything going for him. A typical 'teacher's pet and 'golden boy' of the school football team. There couldn't have been a worse person to say this to Niamh. She felt humiliated and wanted this boy to **DIE!!** When Niamh looked back on this incident years later she realised that his comments were 'sexual harassment' but nothing would have been said or done about him even if she had complained to the teachers.

Xmas 1976 and Niamh was enjoying her holidays, she had had an awful few months worrying about starting her period but Xmas seemed to take her mind of it. Every year on Boxing day the whole family would get wrapped up in warm clothes and take all their dogs on a long walk through the crisp snow. This was to walk off all the Xmas pudding and to get some welcome fresh air after being in doors for the past week playing with new presents. They set off around 2 pm and they walked miles and miles, up hills and along country lanes, they had wonderful rosy cheeks after an hour. The family returned home around 6.30 pm. They were all starving and looking forward to the 'hot pot' supper that Sean had prepared earlier in the day, it just needed heating up. They took off their woolly jackets and rubbed the dogs down with towels. Into the shower Niamh went to warm up and then pop her pyjamas on and settle down to a cosy evening with her family. They all went to bed around 11.pm and were all fast asleep in no time. New dawn, new day, Niamh was woken by the smell of eggs and bacon cooking in the kitchen. "Hmm" she thought "I am starving", so up she got and popped on her dressing gown. "I just need the loo" she shouted down to her Parents. As she sat down on the toilet, she glanced at her underwear, shock horror, for there in her pants was a spot of blood. "NOOOOO" she shrieked, "this can't be happening to me". She felt a sudden panic as though the world had ended. After an hour had passed she was still feeling desperate and bitter that she had to suffer this horrible thing called '**growing up**'. The worse thing on her mind was how was she going to tell her Mother? She had to tell her Mother, what if the blood started coming on fast and she didn't know what to do? So, she plucked up the courage and told her Mother. "Oh darling, come hear" said Kaitlyn and she gave her a big welcome hug. "Don't worry, I will get you a pad and everything will be ok." This was such a relief for Niamh and she instantly felt better in her Mothers protective arms. Well, at least she won`t worry about it anymore, **'it'** had begun and no more nightmares of starting in class.

*Niamh had always resented `growing up`, she thought she could be a child forever.*

# Chapter 29

# THE GOD FATHER

The first time Niamh saw the movie' The God Father' she was entranced. "Imagine the power to have your enemies disappear" she thought to herself, to actually have them `bumped off'. Al Pacino became her hero, she would think about the movie all the time and say to herself "I wonder what Al Pacino would do in this situation"? She fantasied that she belonged to `gangster family', she even imagined herself being Al Pacino`s character Michael Corleone in the movie. She loved the names i.e Sony, Vito, Alfredo Corleone, she thought that she could have come from Sicily because her Mother`s family originated from Italy and settled in Ireland so it could be possible!

Every time someone upset her at school this was her way of coping, imagining that Vito Corleone was her Father and he would `deal' with any scum who threatened her well- being. Niamh`s father Sean would have dealt with the swine`s who hurt her but she never told him because she feared he would be jailed, but in her mind Vito would not be jailed because he was the mafia boss and untouchable.

Niamh`s favourite saying was **"Don't tell me your innocent, because it insults my intelligence"**! This was the statement said in the movie where Michael tells his brutal brother in law that he knew he was responsible for his brother Sony's death and for beating his Sister up. "This was very clever of Michael" she thought "pretending that he had given Carlo a second chance just to get him out of the house quietly, only to be strangled by Michael's men as soon he got into their car, he thought he was being sent to another branch of Casino to work and exiled from New York as punishment". "Brilliant" she said to herself over and over "Brilliant". Everything that Michael did in the movie she scrutinised obsessively, she knew every line and scene and the music was fantastic. She would hum the tune all the time and imagine she was organising some hateful scum bag being 'bumped off'. She planned to go to Hollywood to meet Al Pacino one day, maybe, hopefully. Her Father's Sister lived in New York City and Niamh dreamed of visiting her one day and finding Al Pacino and visit the places were the movie was filmed.

*So, Al Pacino would be Niamh's role model, after Abba though. In her mind, she looked to Al Pacino for protection and she looked to Abba for escapism.*

# Chapter 30

# MEDICATED

By now Niamh had been on her medication for a good 12 months and it seemed to be working, the misery had gone but the rituals were still very much there. The tablets helped immensely but Niamh didn't realise that she was feeling different. It just dawned on her one day that she wasn't suicidal anymore. She took her tablets every day at dinner time but if any 'nosey sod' asked her what the tablets were for, she just said they were vitamins, but one cheeky b**** Marcia Canny said to her "they are not vitamins, what are they"? "How dare this 'thing' question why I am taking tablets" "What the f*** does it have to do with her"? Niamh never swore out loud, her Parents would be very annoyed, but she swore plenty in her mind, it was a way of getting stress out of her system, it also helped her in imagining she was speaking to the hateful people she so despised, she would have great pleasure in screaming what she really wanted to say to them, but she didn't have the confidence. Most of her time spent at the vile place, Niamh was a lamb among Wolves, a little Rabbit trapped in a car's headlights. She was afraid of every- one and trusted no one. The only person she felt any kind of confidence with was Francine, but she had drifted away from her. So, Niamh was coping better on Medication, but her state of mind had been' **put in place'** for the rest of her life. The damage had been done but it was up to the Doctor's to help her manage and deal with her condition.

*There was only a small handful of people that Niamh liked from the vile place and Francine and Jeanie were two of them.*

# Chapter 31

# NAIL POLISH REMOVER

Niamh was very musical, and she enjoyed her Music lessons at school. Listening to Classical Music in the classroom with eyes closed and the blind down while every pupil had to keep quiet, this she thought was relaxing and `civilized'. The Music teacher Mrs.Higham, was the same Music teacher from the Choir, even though Niamh found her aloof, self- important and cold, she didn't hate her. In-fact Music was the only subject along with Art and English Literature that Niamh cared for and she prepared to take these 3 subjects in her final exams. As time went on Mrs. H, seemed to warm to Niamh and showed a caring nature towards her, not much but it was a `human'!

Mrs. H and her `fancy man' Mr. Bonk who she was rumoured to be having an affair with were staging their first Musical … Joseph and his Technicolor Dream coat … You would think it was a Hollywood production the way they drooled over it, it was the talk of the school, but Niamh found it sickly and she detested all the fuss. The way the Mrs. H spewed over how brilliant the cast was. What made Niamh even more sick was the cocky b****** who ridiculed her when he said, "stop playing with your crutch" was the main star, Niamh hated him even more now. She would lay in bed at night and fantasise that the roof fell in on the them all while they were performing.

One Music lesson before the 'big night' Mrs. H was trying to scrape her old nail varnish off without succeeding. "Is anyone going into the town this dinner time" she asked the Music group. Niamh had started to walk into the town at dinner time with another girl who was also a **'misfit'!** They became friends purely through their love of ABBA the Swedish super group. They would stroll into the town centre at dinner times and discuss which Abba songs they loved best. So, this day Mrs. H requested if anybody could go into the town and purchase some nail polish remover for her. "Yes, said Niamh, "I will get some for you". Mrs. H was over the moon, she seemed taken a back that anyone would volunteer for her. She gave Niamh a £5 note and told her to come to the Assembly Hall when she returned from the town. Mrs. H, Mr. B and another teacher Mr. Keel were spending every break time rehearsing and that was were Niamh would find her to give her the nail polish. As Niamh returned to the school after dinner break, she immediately went to find Mrs. H to give her the nail polish and her change. As Niamh glanced through the Hall door window, she could see the group in deep rehearsal, she didn't want to interrupt so she just stood there hoping to catch Mrs. H s eye. On eye contact Mrs. H beckoned to Niamh to enter the Hall, hesitantly that is what she did. She slowly walked into rehearsals and up to Mrs. H with hand out stretched containing the nail polish. Suddenly, Mr. Keel flew into a rage and screamed at Niamh **"What do you want, what the f\*\*\* do you want?** Niamh froze in fear, she was dazed and confused. Mr. K was foaming at the mouth with temper, Niamh was certain that he would **assault** her for interrupting rehearsals. Niamh froze to the spot, she was afraid to move, and she just stood their shaking. She eventually looked at Mrs. H for guidance. Mrs. H was as shocked as Niamh and she just shook her head at Mr. K and beckoned Niamh towards her. "Thank you" is all that she could say, not "sorry for that, I will report Mr. K for that abusive outburst to a female pupil who was on an errand for me. No, the uncaring c*** didn't give a s***. She just wanted her f****** nail polish remover. As for that b****** Mr. Keel, well you can imagine the curse that Niamh tried to inflict on him that night. If Niamh had told her Father Sean how that bad tempered, nasty piece of s*** had spoken to her, he would have destroyed him with one swift left hook.

Looking back on her time at the `vile place' Niamh felt like a coward because she didn't take every one of those b******* to court. If only she had told her Parents! She, might have become rich from the compensation that she should have been in titled to. Or maybe not, looking back she thought that a court case would be pointless because the School Authorities would have `**closed ranks**' and she would have been made out to look a liar!

***Well, Niamh had certainly learned her lesson, never again would she be on friendly terms with any of the teachers, she was right to HATE them ALL.***

# Chapter 32

# HUMAN

September 1979, Niamh was in her last 6 months of the vile place and her heart would pound at the thought of leaving School forever. She had manged to stay in C group but only by a few points in her last tests, though she did wonder if the teachers let her remain in C group because it wouldn't look good on the school **OFSTED** report if they had a relatively intelligent pupil coming from primary school to high school and her grades just kept falling and falling with each assessment. Strange how nobody asked **why?**

This new term was the most important because it was nearly **G.C.S.E** time. Even though Niamh did not choose to take Maths for her final subjects, it was still compulsory to attend the lessons. As you know Niamh was useless at Maths, and that is an understatement. The pupils were all given their new time-tables and find out which teachers were being assigned to which class group. Niamh was dreading who the Maths teacher would be because the previous swine's had all ridiculed her lower than low grades, she was surprised to see a new teacher's name, a Mr. Huller. "What will he be like"? she worried. A few days later she would find out, and to her utter surprise Mr. Huller was the kindest, fairest, liberating teacher she had ever known. This was strange to Niamh, because in her mind she had this **delusion** that all the teachers, were **NOT HUMAN**. This was very real to her, she imagined them as demons from hell, sent to abuse her. She once over heard a teacher discussing to another teacher how they had spent their weekend. Niamh was that shocked that she couldn't stop thinking about. She couldn't believe that teachers went to the cinema, went walking with their dogs, in fact she couldn't believe that they could have a dog or a family for that matter. She really believed that the teachers were demons and the other pupils were their helpers. So, Mr. Huller was a relief for Niamh, she decided that he had been sent to fight the demons and their helpers. The first thing that Niamh noticed about Mr. H was that he smelled nice, a fresh just washed aroma mixed with expensive after- shave. Mr. H was his own man, he didn't mingle with the teacher 'cronies', he stayed in his classroom at lunch time, preferring not to listen to the babblings of the loud mothed, arrogant, pretencious *t\*\*\*\**, who thought they were the best thing since sliced bread. The stuck-up bitches among them and the **holyier-than-thou** hypocrites and the b\*\*\*\*\*\* who thought they were hard men, bragging about how every six- foot boy in the school was afraid of them. Mr. H detested this mentality, he was probably one of the few teachers who chose that choice of career because he had a vocation, he wanted to help kids, not abuse and humiliate them. Mr. H, had respect for his pupils and in return they had mutual respect for him. He could get the best out of any of his class because they felt that he was genuine and most of all Mr. H was HUMAN!

*In later years Mr. H would come back into Niamh's life in an unbelievable twist of fate.*

# Chapter 33

# NEEDLEWORK

One of Niamh's creative subjects were Needlework. She enjoyed the peace and tranquillity of the lesson and she was quite good at it. A week before the exams, and the Needlework teacher Mrs. Shete was all in a stress mode about the girls completing their work before the dead line. Mrs. Shete was a highly- strung woman who blew her top very easily and on many occasions. Niamh thought that she was liked by Mrs. Shete because she was quiet and never give her cheek or hassle. Niamh was very cautious of Mrs. S, because she once witnessed her verbally abusing a girl who had dared to answer her back. The argument seemed to go on for ever and even though the girl stood her ground with the '**witch**' she was clearly traumatised. Mrs. S would go red in the face and the veins in her neck would swell up as though they were about to burst. She hated losing to a pupil and the dispute was practically on the verge of **violence!** When Mrs. S, felt that she was losing the battle, she would resort to the '**cane'.** She would aggressively threaten the girl with her weapon, and rumour had it that she had used it many times. In a nutshell Mrs. S, was a highly strung, nasty, moody woman, who loved assaulting her pupils if they displeased her. The last lesson before all work had to be submitted, Niamh had been working on the sewing machine, she had worked hard to complete her work, ready for the exam board. "Right, stop working and put all your completed work on my desk" shouted Mrs. S. "I hope you have all finished what is required off you, if not I will be very angry". "If you don't do good in this exam it will look bad on me and I won't be happy at all with who -ever hasn't worked hard, if I am to sign on at the dole office next week, then you lot will be joining me ". Threatening words from a Needlework teacher, disgraceful!! After Mrs. S, had verbally **blasted** them all, the girls felt like they were walking on egg shells, the slightest thing would send Mrs. S, into a frenzy. Niamh started to put her sewing machine back into its case, she un plugged the cable and foot pedal. Suddenly one of the girls brushed passed her and caused the foot pedal to fall from her grasp and crash to floor in pieces. After deadly silence for a few seconds Mrs. S, screamed at Niamh," **You, stupid girl,** you are always doing something bloody stupid". Niamh could feel herself going red and she wanted to cry, the hurtful thing was that Niamh never did anything wrong in Needlework. She could do nothing but look helplessly at the `**tyrant'** who had just verbally abused and humiliated her in front of the whole class for something that wasn't her fault. After that Niamh, despised Mrs. S, and she spent the following night putting a curse on her, a heart attack or brain heammorage would have been a vengeful result for Niamh. Yes, she would have liked that very much. How dare that vile woman talk to Niamh like that. She was a disrespectful piece of s*** and Niamh wanted to send her to **HELL!!**

*Poor Niamh could not win in anything she did, sometimes she would be really proud of herself only to be shot down into little pieces.*

# Chapter 34

# FINAL DAYS

Niamh was beside herself with anticipation of what life would be like after School, she sat in her lounge one Saturday watching 'Wimbledon' with her Sister and a close friend, Carol. "I can't wait until my last exam" she said. "As soon as I have finished I will run out of that place and not even glance back at the pile of crap". She didn't even care if she passed any of the 4 exams she was taking. They were English, Music, Needlework and Art. These subjects were a testament of Niamh's potential creativity, if only it had been nurtured and not **ignored.** The friends discussed what they would do after they had finished School, they planned to go to Sweden and find Abba and form their own pop band. The world was Niamh's oyster, but sadly she didn't realise that without good grades she wasn't going anywhere!

The wait up to the first exam came quickly, quicker than Niamh had expected, before she knew it she was sat in the Assembly Hall with the test paper in front of her. She tried her up most for her Parents, but she was eager to get away as soon as the time was up. Because it was exam time, the pupils could leave as soon as they had finished their paper. Niamh thought it was great, it was as though she was free at last. She didn't have to wait for 4.pm anymore, and she was also allowed to stay at home to revise. This was too good to be true she thought. She felt that she was half way to freedom. No more P.E or any other subject or teacher whom she **HATED.** Just before the last exam week, the teachers announced that they were organising a School leavers disco. This meant nothing to Niamh, there was no way she was 'socialising' with **EVIL PEOPLE.** They didn't want to know her 5 years ago, and Niamh certainly didn't want to know them anymore. She still detested everyone in the School with exception from a handful, she thought even if she did want to go to the leavers disco, she feared she would be attacked from one of the scum bags who had bullied her in the past.

The last exam she had was English, and as soon as she had finished she left the hall and grabbed her coat and ran and ran and ran up the long road to the town centre. She didn't say good bye to anyone, she didn't even look back, her heart was pounding. She was certain that some teacher would run after her and drag her back. **"They won't catch me"** she kept saying to herself.

*Once home she was elevated, no more school ever. She kept pinching herself to see if it was real. She had survived the vile place, but not without cost. The mental illness she had developed would stay with her for the rest of her life!*

# Chapter 35

# CONCLUSION

Well, that was just a glimpse into the life of Niamh Conlen. She started off as a normal child but the `vile place changed her for the **worst.** What would she have achieved if she had been allowed to go to the `Covinent' with her best friend? Why was she made to go to a School that did the complete opposite to bringing out her potential? Why was she assaulted several times for something that wasn't her fault, in fact WHY was she assaulted at all? She despised the people that she was forced to spend 5 days a week with and that in turn projected itself into sadistic fantasies of torture and **revenge!** The depression, the delusions, the rituals, the torment, the tears, the desperation, the loss of teenage years, the **HATRED!**

After School, she went to Art College in the near- by town of Rovington. She was happy there but there was also a bully who kept goading her. One day, Niamh thought to her -self **"No you don't, I have left all that behind."** So, she walked right up to this girl nose to nose and asked her what was her problem? The cocky girl s*** herself and just said "I wasn't talking to you". After that the c*** left Niamh alone.

Niamh was amazed at her -self for standing up to this girl who had taken a dislike to, but by now she had convinced herself that she had acquired special powers to make bad things happen to her enemies. She thought that some demon power had decided that she would be an asset to them, if she hated someone enough to wish them harm. Niamh had wished harm on many people at her time at the vile place. She blamed them for everything that went wrong in her life. The convulsions she had suffered in acting out revenge fantasies at night in bed. The fustration she felt because she couldn't do it in real life. "How dare the powers that be deprive me of my revenge" she would chant to herself. She took great pleasure in swearing to herself, it helped to get the hatred out of her system.

After college, Niamh's family moved away to Ireland and they began a new life running a country pub. Everything was going fine until her Father Sean got sick and died! Herself and Mother and Sister returned to England and Niamh did her upmost to support her Mother in grief. She was still on her medication but as her body became '**immune**' to the drugs, Niamh's personality disorder reared its ugly head once again, but that is another story … … Thank you for listening.

Printed in the United States
By Bookmasters